GOURMET
COOKING
for
TWO
by
Beatrice A. Ojakangas

**AUTHOR OF
THE FINNISH COOKBOOK**

CROWN PUBLISHERS, INC., New York

DEDICATED TO
Dick
Cathy
Greg
Susanna

Second Printing, August, 1970

© 1970 by Beatrice A. Ojakangas
Library of Congress Catalog Card Number: 79-93405
Printed in the United States of America
Published simultaneously in Canada by General Publishing Company Limited
Designed by Shari de Miskey

Contents

An Introduction

THE ART OF COOKING FOR TWO

"It's so hard to cook now—there are just the two of us, you see."

This often-heard remark describes a quite common state of affairs. Most of us start out, and end up, in life cooking for only two people. And all too frequently our "cooking for two" degenerates into the monotonous routine of a big meal followed by six or more days of leftovers; or the opposite extreme—all short-order menus. This book was written to help anyone—even a bride—to avoid the monotony that can develop in cooking for two, and to show that "gourmet" cooking is really simple cooking that enhances the flavors of the ingredients you use.

It is easy to break free from the conventional rules of meal planning when you cook for only two. Learn to choose one fine dish, flank it with the simplest of supporting items, and serve it with a flourish. This way, cooking is little work and a great deal of fun. For instance, what you might serve as a first course for a larger group you can serve as a main dish when you are cooking for two.

You can also afford to experiment. I don't mind buying an occasional expensive piece of meat or fish or high-priced shellfish, in such small quantity. And I like to try out new and unusual dishes in small amounts before I serve them to a crowd.

All the recipes in this book have appeared on our own "for two" menus. Where indicated, a recipe can be doubled or tripled for larger groups. Sometimes an adjustment must be made in

1

seasoning or cooking time when increasing a recipe, and I've made note of that, too.

The idea of *Gourmet Cooking for Two* was conceived when, as a student family, my husband and I rarely got a chance to talk to each other without the interruptions of books or children. We began having dinners for two late in the evening, after the children were in bed. This was especially workable because I could prepare for the children the dinners they liked the best, and serve their meal early. They enjoyed the opportunity to choose their favorite spot to eat—indoors, or outdoors picnic-style.

Planning our own more elegant meals gave me the chance to experiment and cook the types of foods that children don't particularly care for but that I might sometime want to serve at a party. There was the added benefit that our meals became as much of an "occasion" for us as dining out. We'd create a setting with candlelight, a tablecloth, crystal, and china (of sorts), and background music from our record collection.

It's a good idea to use some of the "lonesome" articles in your collection of dishes, for these odds and ends can add variety to your table settings. I have a pair of abalone shells that I delight in using for main-dish salads. One day I picked up a couple of old-fashioned, extremely heavy glass sundae-dishes from a close-out at the local hotel and restaurant supply store. I've used them to serve chilled soup and salads as well as dessert sundaes. When we have guests, I use them as holders for celery sticks, nuts, or candy.

Among the recipes in this book are many for basic as well as the more exotic combinations of foods. I hope you will use the recipes freely, adding your own penciled notations to them. Remember that individual tastes vary, even as to the amount of salt in a dish, and so it is important to keep notes about such alterations, especially in seasonings and cooking times.

It is always wise to get the "feel" of a recipe first. Read it through and visualize the process of preparation. Use good judgment and common sense. If the dish looks done before the specified time, it may be that your range is different from mine or that the altitude is different.

Finally, serve your food as attractively as an artist would. Consider color when you choose your menu—and also consider the color of your dishes! Remember, "You eat with your eyes before you eat with your mouth."

Good cooking is really a combination of simple procedures. Anyone who really wants to cook, can!

Happy cooking!

BEATRICE A. OJAKANGAS

A BIT ABOUT UTENSILS AND THINGS

You don't need a burner with a brain or a matched set of cookware to turn out a really fine meal. The long lists of cooking equipment found in many cookbooks have always been confusing to me. For *real* guidance, nose through your mother's kitchen or the kitchen of another experienced cook. Observe which articles have been used often and which have not.

From the beginning of my kitchen life, it has always helped me to visualize the foods I'll be cooking for special meals. I use the same utensil twice in preparing a meal, when that is possible. As my interest in cooking has deepened, I have added more items to my kitchen, but I suspect another cook would classify some of my treasures as junk. When tempted to buy fancy gadgets, remember that some items can do the work of several others. For example, a great variety of mincers and choppers is unnecessary if you have a good French knife.

My cookware consists basically of two saucepans—a one-quart and a two-quart (not matched, for they were wedding gifts)—and a heavy frying pan. These have all been used so much they're about to fall apart. I once had a handy little six-inch frying pan that *did* fall apart, and I replaced it with an omelet pan. One large, rather beat-up stockpot serves numerous purposes. Everything from cabbage to corn on the cob is cooked in that pot, and in between times it holds various small items in the corner cupboard. Actually, I could have replaced these poor old things long ago, but they're so comfortable to work with!

Aside from pots and pans, I keep a few "right arms" around my kitchen: a little whip (about eight inches long), an assortment of wooden spoons, a ten-inch French knife, a six-inch French knife, a boning knife, and a knife with a serrated edge, for cutting bread.

For years I patiently put up with dull knives until one of my brothers explained the principle of knife sharpening to me. It's quite simple: Just think of the knife edge as a V-shape, the point of the V being the cutting edge. To sharpen, just rub the steel or stone downward against the knife blade, to give the blade as pointed a V-shape as possible.

Equipment for measuring is important, too—measuring cups both liquid and dry. Liquid measures are often made of glass, and have the top edge higher than the one-cup mark. To measure liquids, set the cup on a level surface before filling it. Dry measures, usually of metal or plastic, come in sets of four—¼ cup, ⅓ cup, ½ cup, and 1 cup. When measuring dry ingredients, level off the top of the measure with a knife or spatula. Keep a set or two of inexpensive measuring spoons handy on a nail or peg in each of your kitchen work areas.

Mixing bowls are also important, but most people get too many. I find myself using the largest one (three-quart size) most of the time, and next most frequently a two-quart plastic one with a handle and a spout for pouring.

If you bake cookies and pies, you will enjoy using a pastry canvas for rolling out dough. When you're finished, it may still be floury but that doesn't matter. Simply fold it lengthwise, roll it up on your rolling pin, slip the two into a long plastic bag (from a loaf of French bread), and store. You'll almost always use the two together anyway.

A supply of refrigerator dishes with covers is useful, especially the plastic kind that can go into the freezer.

When buying baking pans, you might just as well pass up the cheap tin ones. They will need to be replaced so soon that they are a false economy. One cookie sheet and one jelly-roll pan to begin with are sufficient. (A cookie sheet has no sides, but a jelly-roll pan has sides.)

Molds for gelatin and breads are fun to have and to use. The two kinds can be used almost interchangeably, except for one hitch—if you plan to bake in a salad mold, unless it has a special nonstick coating, you will have to grease and flour it *very* heavily or your baked goods will stick badly. When using a mold for gelatin salad, I like to coat it *very lightly* with salad oil so that the salad will slide out more easily.

To "season" cast-iron molds for baking, before you use them for the first time, rub them heavily with shortening and set in a low oven (250°) for three hours. Remove from oven and cool; then rub the molds with a paper towel to remove any excess grease before storing. The same rule goes for other cast-iron cookware. When washing this type of utensil, don't scour—or you will have to season it again.

Gadgets can be one cook's essential and the next one's junk. Here is my standard group: a knee-action parer, an apple corer, a manual can opener, a wire whip, a punch-type can opener, and a garlic press. However, electrical gadgets are becoming more and more prevalent in the well-equipped kitchen. The electric mixer, blender, toaster, coffeepot, frypan, waffle iron, and grill are probably the most popular. They were all invented to be laborsavers— but they save no labor unless you *use* them. The blender is my favorite because it's a "mess saver." I use it for making crumbs, chopping onions, puréeing foods, and so on.

Another fine appliance is the radarange. Once you have learned its virtues—how quickly it can thaw the chicken you forgot to remove from the freezer, or heat a cup of coffee (in thirty seconds), or heat one meal at a time for dinner stragglers, or cook corn on the cob (in two minutes *without* water)—it becomes—indispensable. A radarange comes in two basic types: as a freestanding unit and as part of the regular cooking range. Both types have their virtues. Which one you choose will depend on your budget, the space in your kitchen, whether you'd like to take it along on boating or other vacation trips, or whether you want to move it around in the house. Radaranges have differences in wavelength and strength that affect cooking times. You can get the best information on them directly from the companies that produce them.

Menus for Two

Planning gourmet menus for two can be exciting. Just consider the thousands of possible dishes that might be served. However, gourmet cooking for two need not involve a lot of fussy "extras"; you can concentrate on the *pièce de résistance*; the accompaniments for it can be very simple.

The various chapters of this book present many dishes to choose from. The menus that follow are merely suggestions, though we ourselves have enjoyed these particular combinations. Adapt and change items as freely as you wish. Just remember to think of the main course first and the accompaniment second.

Some of the menu suggestions are specific. Some are offered in a different manner—so that you can choose from a variety of "go-withs" according to the availability of the ingredients, your budget, and your time.

Refer to the index to find the recipes for those dishes listed in capital letters.

PICNIC IDEAS

Picnics for two are a delightful switch from the usual. The paraphernalia for two is so much less bulky than for a group, you can afford to use real dishes, if you like!

I. TOTE ALONG A SOUP

Serve it hot or cold from a vacuum bottle. Serve any of the following:

CREAM CONSOMMÉ
GREEN PEA CONSOMMÉ
BEAN SOUP
CLAM CHOWDER
SPLIT PEA SOUP
GAZPACHO
MINESTRONE
VICHYSSOISE

Also take along a choice of:

Bread
Sesame crackers and cheese
HERBED ENGLISH MUFFINS
Crusty hard rolls

Relishes
Olives, sweet gherkins, tiny pickled ears of corn (available in
gourmet shops), green pepper strips, zucchini sticks (raw), cucumber sticks, cherry tomatoes

Beverages
Chilled white wine
Hot coffee or tea

Dessert
FRESH FRUIT AND CHEESE
MELON WITH PORT
Cookies or cake (homemade or bought)

II. PORK TENDERLOIN IN PASTRY

Make it at home and chill well. Slice and pack as you would
sandwiches. Serve with:

Condiments
Hot mustard, hot catsup, chutney

Salads
(pack in paper cups)
SPICY OYSTER COCKTAIL SALAD
AUTUMN SALAD
MANDARIN CARROT SALAD
SCANDINAVIAN TOMATO SALAD

Desserts that go well
ICED CANTALOUPE
GINGERED PLUMS

Beverages
Chilled California Rosé
Coffee or tea

III. BACON, EGG, AND TOMATO SALAD

Make and chill at home; pack in disposable salad bowls. Choose from the following finger foods:

Breads
Italian-style breadsticks
HERBED BREAD
Scandinavian crisp bread

Pickles and such
Fat juicy "half" dills (a kind of dill pickle found in the refrigerated cabinets at groceries—they're only half processed, and taste like homemade ones)
Pickled cherry peppers
Assorted cheese sticks (cut into sticks at home)

Desserts
Fresh fruit and pound cake

IV. WINE-MARINATED PICNIC BURGERS

If you do not have a small portable grill, improvise one with a metal cake pan and cake rack. Carry fluid-soaked charcoal in a jar. Light 6 to 8 pieces. Serve burgers with:

Breads
Hard sesame rolls (from bakery)
Sliced French bread
MOLASSES RYE ROLLS
(use recipe given for Molasses Rye Bread, but shape into rolls instead of a loaf)

Condiments
Mustard, relish, chopped onion

Relishes
Dill pickles, carrots, celery fans, and tomato slices

Dessert
POTS DE CRÈME and COOKIES

BREAKFASTS AND BRUNCHES FOR TWO

Brunches offer a latitude in menu planning that you get at hardly any other time of day. Breakfasts can be even simpler, or as elaborate as an eight-course dinner. I suggest the simplest kind because that is the most practical for today's mode of living. Here are some good combinations. To add elegance for a special occasion, try serving a sparkling grape juice, sparkling catawba, sparkling cider, or even champagne!

BUTTERED PINEAPPLE SPEARS
MEXICAN OMELET   Danish pastry (from bakery)
Sparkling Beverage
Coffee

Chilled Sparkling Cider
FRENCH EGG CASSEROLE   Toasted English Muffins
Coffee

Strawberries in Champagne
FRIED CHEESE SLICES   Rye Toast
Coffee

Sliced Oranges with Mint
RUSSIAN CHEESE PATTIES   Cinnamon Rolls (bakery)
Coffee

GREEN GRAPES WITH SOUR CREAM
POPOVERS   Marmalade   Sweet Butter
Sparkling Rosé
Hot coffee

Sliced Bananas in Fresh Orange Juice
SHRIMP-FILLED PUFFS   Coffee

LUNCHES, SUPPERS, AND MIDNIGHT SUPPERS

These "light meals" are the most fun of all because they're so
unorthodox, even from the standpoint of timing. They're also easy
on the cook. Choose a "little main dish" from that chapter. Serve
it with a complementary salad or hot bread if you wish—or maybe
both. I might also suggest that you shop the freezer cabinet of
your grocery store. New frozen entrées come on the market fre-

quently—everything from the elegance of lobster and crab to variety in vegetable dishes. Let some of these convenience foods spark up your dinners for two sometimes.

The recipes for the dishes suggested in the following menus are given elsewhere in this book. Here we suggest a main course, and give you the freedom of choosing the accompaniments according to your tastes, your needs at the time, the available ingredients, and your pocketbook:

I. OCEAN PERCH THERMIDOR

Salads

TOMATO AND DILL PICKLE SALAD
HEARTS OF LETTUCE WITH LEMON AND CREAM
FRESH BEEFSTEAK TOMATO SALAD

Breads

HOT POPOVERS

Scandinavian wafers (purchased)
Hot crusty French bread (purchased)

Dessert

FRENCH FRUIT CROÛTES

Sugared fresh fruit in season

II. SCALLOPS IN CHEESE SAUCE

Salads

COMBINATION SALAD WITH BROWNED BUTTER
BASIC GREEN SALAD with choice of dressing
AVOCADO TOMATO SALAD

Bread

Hard rolls (purchased)
Assorted crackers or crisp breads (purchased)

Dessert

STRAWBERRIES FLAMBÉ
FLAMBÉED PEACHES
ORANGE MARMALADE SOUFFLÉ

III. TUNA SALAD IN PASTRY SHELLS

Dessert

Fruit platter
GINGERED PLUMS
ORANGE-BROILED BANANAS WITH ICE CREAM

IV. SWISS CHEESE FONDUE

Salad

BASIC GREEN SALAD
GREEN SALAD PARMESAN
CAESAR SALAD

Dessert

Chilled fresh fruit
WINTER DESSERT
GREEN GRAPES WITH SOUR CREAM

V. QUICHE LORRAINE

Salad

ICEBERG LETTUCE AMANDINE
BELGIAN ENDIVE SALAD
ASPARAGUS SALAD

Dessert

CHANTILLY FIGS
BAKED STUFFED APPLES
PEARS CARDINAL

VI. CHICKEN LIVERS AVOCADO

Salad

BASIC GREEN SALAD
QUICK TOMATO SALAD
ZUCCHINI SALADE FRANÇOISE

Dessert

PEACH HONEY TARTS
STRAWBERRIES WITH SOUR CREAM

DINNER BY CANDLELIGHT

There are times for private celebration. There are also times when you feel in the mood for a particularly romantic meal. These are occasions when you should dine by candlelight, with music, and at a leisurely pace. For such extra-special meals, try to blend the right wine with the right food. It is thrilling to find a real marriage of flavors—and you can do it relatively inexpensively when you choose the fine California varietal wines. They are available in half bottles or tenths occasionally, just the right amount for a dinner for two.

To bring out the real bouquet of a wine, open it about half an hour before serving. Most authorities agree that red wine must be allowed this breathing time, but I have found that white wines—especially the very fine ones with a flowery bouquet—also seem to "blossom" when allowed a breathing time. Of course, the white wine should be kept in an ice bucket to keep it chilled during this time.

STANDING RIB FOR TWO
Baked Idaho Potato   Sour Cream and Chives
FRESH BEEFSTEAK TOMATO SALAD
Hot French Bread   Butter
BANANAS AU RHUM

California Cabernet Sauvignon (serve at room temperature)

MUSHROOM CONSOMMÉ
ROSEMARY RACK OF LAMB   WHEAT PILAF
Orange and Grapefruit Salad
Fresh Strawberries   CHANTILLY SAUCE

California Zinfandel (serve at room temperature)

TOMATO-POTATO SOUP
CRISP SPINACH SALAD
BROCHETTE OF PORK TENDERLOIN
GARLIC MUSHROOMS
STRAWBERRIES WITH QUICK CUSTARD CREAM
California Pinot Noir (serve at room temperature)

CREAM CONSOMMÉ
TOMATO AND DILL PICKLE SALAD
Barbecued Hanging Tenderloin
GREEN BEANS WITH GARLIC
Cantaloupe with Cream
California Zinfandel (serve at room temperature)

CELERY SOUP
MEDITERRANEAN SALAD
VEAL SCALLOPINE
NEW POTATOES WITH HERBS
VANILLA ICE CREAM WITH GALLIANO
California Green Hungarian (serve chilled)

HERB CONSOMMÉ
HEARTS OF LETTUCE WITH FRENCH DRESSING
ENTRECÓTE ROQUEFORT
WILD RICE WITH PEAS
POTS DE POMMES
California Cabernet Sauvignon (serve at room temperature)

CRACKED CRAB
LEMON BUTTER   HOT MAYONNAISE
GREEN SALAD WITH FRENCH DRESSING
French Bread
Fresh Pears, Grapes
California Sauvignon Blanc (serve chilled)

CRAB NEWBURG IN PATTY SHELLS
AVOCADO-TOMATO SALAD
GRAND MARNIER SOUFFLÉ
California Folle Blanche (serve chilled)

SIMPLE GAZPACHO
CHICKEN BREASTS MILANESE
ZUCCHINI AU GRATIN
ITALIAN SALAD
QUICK CUSTARD CREAM
California Grenache Rosé (served chilled)

FRESH MUSHROOM SOUP
PLANKED LAMB CHOPS WITH VEGETABLES
WILTED LETTUCE SALAD
Pineapple Sherbet with Crème de Menthe
California Gamay (serve at room temperature)

MOCK TURTLE SOUP
CAULIFLOWER SALAD
PLANKED PORTERHOUSE STEAK
SPINACH WITH MUSHROOMS
MEXICAN CHOCOLATE PUDDING
California Pinot Noir (serve at room temperature)

CHILLED CURRIED SOUP
GREEN BEAN SALAD
FLANK STEAK BROIL
Cherry Tomatoes
KAHLÙA SOUFFLÉ
California Zinfandel (serve at room temperature)

GREEN PEA CONSOMMÉ
ICEBERG LETTUCE AMANDINE
COQUILLES SAINT-JACQUES WITH MUSHROOMS
CRÈME BRÛLÉE
California Pinot Chardonnay (serve chilled)

SHRIMP BISQUE
LAMB CHOPS TARRAGON   BROILED MUSHROOMS
SCANDINAVIAN TOMATO SALAD
Vanilla Ice Cream with Cointreau
California Gamay (serve at room temperature)

SOLE FLORENTINE
ASPARAGUS WITH DILL SAUCE
LETTUCE AND EGG SALAD
CHOCOLATE SOUFFLÉ

California Gray Riesling (serve chilled)

BROCCOLI CREAM SOUP
SOLE OR PIKE FILLETS WITH MUSHROOMS
GREEN BEANS WITH BACON
LETTUCE AND TOMATO SALAD
SALZBURGER NOCKERLS

California Pinot Chardonnay (serve chilled)

CHICKEN CUTLETS, RUSSE
FEATHERED RICE
MANDARIN CARROT SALAD

Pears and Provolone

California Traminer (serve chilled)

TOMATO CONSOMMÉ
BEEF STROGANOFF
WHEAT PILAF WITH MUSHROOMS
HOT BACON AND LETTUCE SALAD

Cherry Ice Cream with Jamaica Rum

California Pinot Noir (serve at room temperature)

Great Soups

If I were to try to describe a soup, there would always be someone to prove me wrong. There are soups, broths, potages, stews, consommés, and so on. Here, I have taken the liberty of classifying as "soup" an offering of dishes that must be served in a bowl or soup plate, and eaten, usually, with a soup spoon.

In a world oriented to the can opener, particularly when it comes to soup, it is an incredible paradox that homemade soups are so easy to make. You almost can't go wrong! You can take liberties, change ingredients, change the routine, even do half the preparation at one time and leave the rest for another, and still the soup will not suffer. The only rule here is that you taste and correct the seasoning.

I have found that most frozen canned soups are of extremely high quality, and I like to keep a couple on hand for a quick meal. They're also excellent bases to add to, or they can be used as a sauce.

The soup recipes in this chapter begin with the clear, thin consommés and progress to the heartier ones filled with bits of meat, vegetable, pastas, and so on. I like to serve an aromatic consommé as the start for a meal, but something as hearty as the Brussels Sprouts Bisque is enough to *be* a meal!

Once you've discovered the greatness of homemade soups, you'll want to enjoy them often. You may even be tempted to splurge on a soup tureen so that you can serve soups at parties with real elegance.

In the recipes that follow, those that can be doubled or tripled without other necessary changes are designated with an asterisk (*).

HOMEMADE CHICKEN BROTH

Chicken broth is a basic to many recipes. You can purchase it in canned form, use a bouillon cube (not so desirable), or make it from scratch, which is not a hard job. Here are basic directions:

To make 2 or 3 quarts of broth, choose a large pot (about 8- to 10-quart size). Put in 2 to 3 quarts of uncooked chicken bones cut up into about 3-inch pieces (turkey bones can be used the same way), along with the giblets from the chicken. Cover with cold water. Add 2 cut-up carrots, 2 cut-up stalks of celery, 2 cut-up medium-size onions, 2 whole cloves of garlic (optional), ¼ teaspoon thyme, a bay leaf, and several sprigs of parsley. Simmer, partially covered, for 4 to 5 hours. Keep the simmering point so low that the broth does not boil over. Skim when necessary to remove any scum that may form. If the liquid boils down too much, add more water. After simmering, cool and then strain the broth through a fine sieve or cheesecloth. Chill in the refrigerator to solidify fat for removal. Store in quart jars in the refrigerator, or freeze small portions of the broth for later use. Some can be frozen in ice-cube trays for use as small cubes to flavor sauces or soups conveniently.

*CREAM CONSOMMÉ

2 cups chicken broth (canned   ½ cup heavy cream
  or homemade)   2 tablespoons cooking sherry
1 egg yolk, beaten   salt and pepper to taste

Heat the broth to boiling. Beat the egg yolk and cream together; slowly stir it into the hot broth. Add sherry; taste and then add salt and pepper. (Don't reboil the soup after the egg and cream mixture is added or it may curdle.) Serve steaming hot.

*HERB CONSOMMÉ

Simple as it is, this one has a delightful aromatic quality. The base is chicken broth, which you can buy canned, or prepare it in your own kitchen as directed in the recipe for Homemade Chicken Broth.

2 cups hot chicken broth   2 slices lemon
2 tablespoons *each* chopped
    fresh parsley, chervil, chives,
    and tarragon

Have the broth steaming hot. Add the herbs and let stand, covered, for 3 to 5 minutes. Strain. Serve with a lemon slice in each bowl.

*TOMATO CONSOMMÉ

The rosy-red color of this elegant soup makes it ideal as a starter to a romantic meal.

2 medium-sized tomatoes,   2 cups chicken broth, canned or
    peeled   fresh
                         salt and pepper to taste

To peel the tomatoes, dip them in boiling water for a few seconds and then slip off the skins. Cut in half, press out seeds, and dice into about ½-inch cubes. Bring broth to a boil. Add diced tomatoes, remove from heat immediately, and season to taste with salt and freshly ground pepper. (We prefer to keep a pepper grinder on the table and add pepper to suit our own tastes.)

*CHICKEN CONSOMMÉ WITH SHERRY

2 eggs   1 tablespoon lemon juice
2 tablespoons sherry   2 cups hot chicken broth
                    salt and pepper to taste

Beat the eggs, sherry, and lemon juice together until they are well blended. Heat the broth just until steaming; then slowly add the egg mixture, beating vigorously with a whip to make a creamy-looking soup. Taste, and add salt and pepper. Serve hot, garnished with a sprig of parsley.

*MUSHROOM CONSOMMÉ

This one is excellent accompanied by an assortment of cheeses and hard and soft rye breads, with a fresh fruit salad for dessert.

¼ pound fresh mushrooms,   10½-ounce can beef broth, di-
   chopped   luted as directed on label
                    butter

Simmer the mushrooms in the beef broth for 15 minutes. Serve steaming hot with a dab of butter in each bowl.

*CLAM CHOWDER

½ pint (1 cup) fresh clams (or   1 small potato, diced
   frozen, thawed)   1 cup boiling water
1 tablespoon butter   1 cup hot milk
1 chopped green onion   salt and pepper to taste

Chop the clams. Melt the butter in a pan and add the onion, potato, and water. Simmer 20 minutes or until the potato is tender. Add clams; cook 3 minutes. Add the milk and heat but don't boil. Add salt and pepper to taste. Serve with crisp crackers.

MANHATTAN CLAM CHOWDER

Follow the preceding recipe, substituting an additional cup of water or a cup of clam broth or a cup of stewed tomatoes for the milk.

*BACON AND SPINACH SOUP

¼ pound sliced bacon	1 small onion, sliced
pinch of rosemary	salt and pepper
1 bunch (1 pound) fresh spinach, well washed and drained	2 cups milk

Cook the bacon in a large frying pan until crisp; drain off all but about 1 tablespoon of the drippings. Add rosemary, spinach, and onion; toss with the bacon until cooked through. Put the mixture in a blender and process until smooth. Add salt and pepper to taste. Add milk until the soup is of the desired thickness. Blend again, taste, and correct seasoning; then pour it into a pan and heat until steaming. (This soup can be made ahead and reheated just before serving.)

*CHILLED BORSCHT

The unusually rich and creamy flavor of this soup comes from the beaten egg that is added in a rather unorthodox manner—it is not cooked. Though very quick and easy to make, this borscht has an authentic Old World flavor.

16-ounce can julienne or sliced beets	2 teaspoons fresh lemon juice
1 egg, well beaten	2 tablespoons commercial sour cream
2 teaspoons sugar	chopped chives for garnish

Pour the beets and their juice into a mixing bowl. Add the beaten egg, sugar, and lemon juice, mixing well. Chill. Pour into serving bowls and top with sour cream and chives.

*GREEN PEA CONSOMMÉ

2 cups chicken broth (canned   1 tablespoon instant minced
  or homemade)   onion
1 cup fresh or frozen green peas   pinch of tarragon
                              butter

Heat the chicken broth to boiling, and add the peas, onion, and tarragon. Cover and simmer for 15 minutes. Serve hot with a pat of butter on each serving.

*BEAN SOUP

Bean Soup on a wintery day, served steaming in bowls, coupled with a sandwich or meat enclosed in pastry (such as the Pork Tenderloin in Pastry), is pure and simple pleasure for two.

½ cup dry navy or other small   1 small bay leaf
  white beans   1 small whole onion, quartered
3 cups water   1 ham hock
1½ teaspoons sugar   salt, pepper, and nutmeg to taste

Put the beans, water, sugar, bay leaf, onion, and ham hock into a pot and bring to a boil. Lower heat so that the liquid boils slowly. Cook 3½ hours, or until the soup becomes milky in color. Skim if necessary. Check the soup and stir it often. Add more water when necessary as the liquid boils down. Taste and add salt, pepper, and a dash of nutmeg. For best flavor, refrigerate overnight before serving; this seems to meld the flavors.

*CHINESE EGG FLOWER SOUP (or Egg Drop Soup)

Whether or not you plan an entire Oriental meal, this soup is a perfect starter. For a light meal, couple it with hot egg rolls purchased frozen or from a local Chinese restaurant or delicatessen, if you're fortunate enough to have a good one nearby.

1 egg   chopped parsley
2 cups rich chicken broth   for garnish
  (canned or homemade)

Beat the egg with a fork. Bring the broth to the simmering
point, remove from heat, and slowly drizzle in the beaten egg,
stirring slowly. The egg should become stringy-looking rather than
making the soup appear milky. Garnish with parsley and serve hot.

*CELERY SOUP

3 stalks celery   salt and pepper to taste
2 cups beef broth   toasted croutons
                     butter

Cut the celery into slices about ¼ inch thick. Bring the broth
to a boil, add the celery, and simmer for 15 minutes. Taste, and
then add salt and pepper. Serve with toasted croutons, and float
a pat of butter on top of each serving.

*CREAM OF FRESH MUSHROOM SOUP

¼ pound fresh mushrooms   1 egg yolk, slightly beaten
1 tablespoon butter   2 tablespoons sherry or 1 tea-
1 tablespoon flour   spoon lemon juice
1½ cups milk   salt and pepper to taste

Separate the caps and stems of the mushrooms. Slice the caps
and chop the stems. Heat the butter in a saucepan. Add the mushrooms and cook 5 minutes over medium heat, stirring. Sprinkle
the flour over the mushrooms. Add milk and stir until blended.
Cook until slightly thickened. Blend egg yolk and sherry or lemon
juice. Stir into soup. Taste and add salt and pepper. Serve hot.

*BROCCOLI CREAM SOUP

If you have a blender, this is just one of the things you can do with it. It is also handy for making other kinds of vegetable-cream soups.

1 cup raw broccoli, chopped	dash of nutmeg
½ cup water	½ teaspoon salt
¾ cup milk	2 egg yolks
1 teaspoon sugar	2 tablespoons lemon juice
	sour cream

Wash the broccoli well. Put it and the water into a pan, cover, and cook 5 minutes. Add the milk, sugar, nutmeg, and salt. Process in a blender until smooth, or press through a fine wire sieve to purée. Return to cooking pot. Cover and cook over lowest heat for 5 minutes. Don't boil! Serve steaming hot, and pass a bowl of sour cream at the table.

*DANDELION SOUP

When you're out for a stroll on a bright spring day, collect some young dandelion leaves. (Be sure that the dandelions you collect have not been sprayed with dangerous poisons or weed killers.) The flavor of dandelion is much like that of spinach, and this soup is a "tasty treat to set before the king"—in the spring.

2 cups young dandelion greens	1 teaspoon salt
1 large potato	1 egg yolk
2 cups water	1 tablespoon melted butter
	toasted croutons

Wash the dandelion greens very well, picking out the tough ones, cutting off any tough ends. Drain and chop fine. Peel and dice the potato. Put greens, potato, and water into a pan, and simmer 30 minutes or until the potato is done. Add the salt. Press through a sieve, or whirl in a blender until soup is smooth. Blend the egg yolk and butter, and slowly add them to the soup, beating well. Do not boil the soup. Serve hot, garnished with the croutons.

*SUMMER VEGETABLE SOUP

A great soup made in quantity, but of course it can wear out its welcome if you must eat it every night for a week. So here's our "for two" version:

2 small carrots, peeled and diced	boiling water
½ cup fresh shelled peas	salt and pepper to taste
4 new potatoes the size of golf balls, or 1 large one, quartered	1 teaspoon sugar
	1 tablespoon butter, melted
	2 teaspoons flour
	1½ cups milk
½ cup fresh string beans, cut in ½-inch pieces	1 egg yolk
2 small radishes, peeled and cut in half	¼ cup heavy cream
	½ cup small cooked shrimp or diced cooked ham

parsley for garnish

Prepare the carrots, peas, potatoes, string beans, and radishes, and put them into a pan. Cover with boiling water (don't drown them; just add enough water so that the top layer is barely covered). Add salt (½ to 1 teaspoon) and pepper if you like, plus the sugar. Simmer for 10 minutes or until the vegetables are barely tender (not mushy). Combine the butter, flour, milk, and egg yolk, and beat lightly with a fork. Stir the mixture into the cooked vegetables. Add the cream and ham, and heat through (don't boil). Serve the soup garnished with parsley.

*GERMAN BEER SOUP

12-ounce can flat beer   dash of salt
1 cup beef broth (canned)   dash of cinnamon
1 tablespoon lemon juice   pinch of sugar
                1 tablespoon cornstarch

Open the beer well ahead, and let it go flat. Heat the beer and beef broth with the lemon juice, salt, cinnamon, and sugar until simmering. Hold at simmering point for 10 minutes for the flavors to blend. Mix the cornstarch with a small amount of water, enough to make a smooth paste, and stir it into the hot beer mixture. Cook gently until thickened and smooth. Serve hot.

*AMERICAN MEAT SOUP

½ pound stewing beef   pinch of thyme
water   ½ bay leaf
¼ cup rice   salt and pepper to taste
1 onion, chopped   2 egg yolks
                parsley or dill for garnish

Cut the stewing beef into small pieces. Put these into a pan, barely cover with cold water, and bring to a boil. Cover and simmer for an hour or until the meat is tender. Remove scum if any appears. Add the rice, onion, thyme, bay leaf, and salt and pepper to taste. Cook gently for 30 minutes, stirring occasionally. Remove from heat. Beat the egg yolks with a small amount of the soup stock, mixing well. Blend egg-yolk mixture into the soup, stirring vigorously. The soup should be quite thick. Serve garnished with parsley or dill.

Note: This soup can be made ahead, or you can cook only the meat ahead, refrigerate it, and complete cooking the soup the next day.

*BULGARIAN SELSKA TCHORBA

1 medium-sized onion, chopped	1 egg yolk
2 cups water	salt and pepper to taste
1 small celery root, shredded	1 tablespoon butter

Cook the onion in the water until it is soft, about 7 minutes. Press through a fine sieve or process in a blender until smooth. Return to the pan; add the celery root and bring to a boil. Cook until celery root shreds are tender. Pour a small amount of the soup into a cup. Add the egg yolk, and beat until blended. Put the egg-yolk mixture into the soup and stir until soup is thickened. Taste; then add salt and pepper. Serve with butter floating on top of the soup.

*SIMPLE GAZPACHO

You may want to serve this soup in cocktail glasses or punch cups for a party (of course, this means you have increased the recipe according to the number to be served). Otherwise, try it first as an opener to a meal. The garnishes are added to taste at the table by each diner.

16-ounce can tomato juice	garnishes of diced green
1 tablespoon lemon juice	peppers, onion, cucumbers,
1 teaspoon olive oil	and toasted croutons
salt and pepper to taste	

Blend the tomato juice, lemon juice, olive oil, and salt and pepper together. Cover and chill until serving time. The longer the chilling, the better the flavor. Serve the garnishes separately in small bowls, to be spooned into the soup cup or bowl at the table.

*ICED TOMATO SOUP

When fresh tomatoes are available "vine ripened," this soup really tastes the best.

2 large ripe tomatoes, peeled and chopped	1 tablespoon tomato paste
½ small white onion, chopped	2 teaspoons flour
¼ cup water	1 chicken bouillon cube dissolved in 1 cup water
dash of salt and pepper	⅓ cup heavy cream

Combine the tomatoes, onion, ¼ cup water, salt, and pepper in a saucepan. Cook over moderate heat for 5 minutes. Combine the tomato paste and flour, and add it to the chicken bouillon. Stir this mixture into the hot mixture. Simmer gently for 3 minutes. Press the soup through a sieve or process in a blender until puréed. Chill thoroughly. Just before serving, add the cream. Taste; add more salt if necessary. Garnish with a thin slice of tomato if you wish.

ANDALUSIAN GAZPACHO

This is a refreshing soup—one to serve on a hot summer day. If you have a blender, it is very simple to do. (Or a food mill will serve the purpose.)

2 medium-sized tomatoes	1 tablespoon lemon juice
1 small onion	salt and pepper to taste
1 small green pepper	sliced fresh cucumber for garnish
1 teaspoon salad oil or olive oil	toasted croutons for garnish
dash of garlic salt	

Wash and peel the tomatoes. Peel and chop the onion. Remove seeds from the green pepper. Put tomatoes, onion, green pepper, oil, garlic, salt, and lemon juice into the blender container. Process until smooth. Season to taste with salt and pepper. (You may wish to add a pinch of sugar, too.) Chill in the refrigerator. Serve garnished with sliced fresh cucumber and toasted croutons.

To serve four: Double all quantities, but process the soup in two batches.

To serve six: Triple all quantities, but process the soup in three batches.

*SOPA CATALANA

1 large onion, sliced	1 stalk celery, chopped
3 tablespoons olive oil or bacon	¼ cup dry white wine
drippings	2 cups chicken broth or water
1 cup diced ham	pinch each of thyme and parsley
2 medium-sized tomatoes,	pinch of nutmeg
peeled and quartered	1 potato, peeled and diced
salt to taste	

Sauté the onion in the olive oil or bacon drippings until golden (use the same pan you will make the soup in). Add the ham, tomatoes, and celery, then the wine, and bring just to the boiling point. Stir in the chicken broth or water. Add the seasonings and potato. Simmer for 15 to 20 minutes. Taste; then add salt. Serve hot.

*CHILLED CURRIED SOUP

2 cups chicken broth	1 egg yolk
½ cup cooked chicken, cubed	½ cup cream
¼ to ½ teaspoon curry powder	salt to taste

Bring the broth to a boil. Add the chicken and curry powder. Blend the egg yolk and cream together and beat vigorously into the hot mixture. *Don't* boil, but cook for one minute, stirring. Taste; then add salt. Chill before serving.

SPLIT PEA SOUP

Here's a soup where tastes will vary, and appetites as well.

¼ cup split peas (the quick-cooking kind)	1 small onion, diced
	water
1 stalk celery, cut in 1-inch pieces	1 ham shank or hock
	salt and pepper to taste
whole allspice	

Put the peas, celery, and onion into a pan and cover with water. Add the ham shank or hock. Simmer slowly for an hour, adding more water if necessary to keep the peas moist. Add salt and pepper to taste, and drop into the pot 3 or 4 whole allspice. Simmer again for an hour or so. Longer simmering produces richer flavor. This soup will be on the thin side. It can be thickened with a paste made of equal parts of flour and water and stirred into the hot soup; cook until thickened to your taste. (We prefer the thinner soup as a first course, the thicker soup for lunch.)

For four servings: Double all quantities except ham; double that if you wish, but just one shank or hock will be sufficient.

For six servings: Triple the quantities, but the same rule holds for the ham—add more or less according to taste.

*CREAM OF FRESH PEA SOUP

1 cup fresh shelled peas (or frozen, thawed)	1 egg yolk, beaten
	1 tablespoon butter
¾ cup water	salt and pepper to taste
1 cup light cream or half-and-half	

Cook the peas in the water for 7 minutes. Process in a blender until smooth or press through wire strainer to purée. Blend the cream with the beaten egg yolk, and add to the pea purée. Cook over low heat for 5 minutes, stirring. Taste; then add butter and salt and pepper.

*CHEESE SOUP

1 medium-sized potato	½ cup sour cream
about 2 cups water	1 tablespoon butter
¼ cup grated Parmesan cheese	salt and pepper to taste

parsley for garnish

Peel and dice the potato. Put it in a pan with water to cover, and cook until tender (about 15 minutes). Press potato through wire sieve or process in a blender to make a purée. Return purée to the cooking broth and add the Parmesan cheese, sour cream, butter, and salt and pepper. Heat until steaming hot, but do not boil. Garnish with parsley, and serve.

*CONSOMMÉ AU VIN

This elegant-sounding soup is really very simple to prepare, though it doesn't taste that way.

2 cups canned beef broth or consommé (diluted according to label directions)	½ cup dry red wine, such as a burgundy or claret
	dash of salt and pepper

2 slices lemon

Bring the beef broth or consommé to a boil. Add the wine, salt, and pepper. Serve steaming hot with a slice of lemon in each bowl.

*AVOCADO SOUP

This is a spectacular soup, one ladies especially enjoy because it's different—for impressing Aunt Minerva or your mother-in-law.

1 cup chicken broth	salt and pepper to taste
2 tablespoons flour	1 medium-size avocado
1 cup light cream	4 sliced ripe olives
lemon wedges	

Combine the chicken broth and flour in a pan. Bring to simmering over medium heat, stirring until smooth and thickened. Add the light cream, and salt and pepper to taste. Dice the avocado and add it to the hot soup along with the sliced olives. Remove from heat. Be careful not to boil or hold the soup at high temperature too long, as the avocado will take on a bitter flavor. Serve piping hot. Squeeze lemon into the soup as desired.

*CREAM OF SPINACH SOUP

Serve this soup as a first course or with a sandwich for lunch; or thin it with milk and serve in a mug as a late-evening snack or after skiing or a Sunday-afternoon hike. If you must, you can substitute frozen spinach for the fresh.

½ pound fresh spinach (or	1 tablespoon flour
1 package frozen chopped	dash of thyme
spinach)	dash of nutmeg
1 tablespoon butter	¼ teaspoon salt
1 cup light cream	sour cream
toasted croutons	

Wash the spinach well to remove sand. Trim off the root ends. Melt the butter in a saucepan and add the spinach. Cover and steam for 5 minutes on high heat. Transfer to the blender and process until smooth, or press through a strainer to make a purée. Return to the pan. Mix the cream in, add the flour, thyme, nutmeg, and salt. Cook over medium heat, stirring until slightly thickened. Add milk if necessary to thin the soup. Serve hot, and spoon sour cream into each serving; garnish with toasted croutons.

*QUICK MINESTRONE

A good Minestrone, made the traditional way, is one of our favorite soups. Often, we make a whole meal of it. But this quick version, though not as authentic, is high on flavor, and saves time in the kitchen, too.

1 slice bacon, diced	8-ounce can kidney beans,
1 small onion, chopped	drained
1 small clove garlic, minced	¼ teaspoon *each* basil and
½ cup long macaroni, broken	oregano
into 2-inch pieces	1 tablespoon fresh parsley,
2 cups beef broth	chopped
2 cups water	salt and pepper to taste
10-ounce package frozen mixed	Parmesan cheese
vegetables	

Fry the bacon in a 2-quart pan until almost crisp. Drain off all but about 1 tablespoon of the fat; then add the onion and garlic. Cook, stirring, about 2 minutes, or until the onion is limp. Add the macaroni and stir until it is hot and begins to show a "chalky" white color (about 3 minutes over medium heat). Add the beef broth and water, bring to boiling, and let boil uncovered for 5 minutes. Add the vegetables and cook another 5 minutes. Then season with the basil, oregano, parsley, salt, and pepper. Cover, turn heat to low, and allow to "mellow" for 20 to 30 minutes before serving. Serve soup with Parmesan cheese to spoon into the individual servings at the table.

*BRUSSELS SPROUTS BISQUE

Fancy—but what a good way to get an extra vegetable into the menu! With a meat sandwich or salad, you've got it made.

10-ounce package frozen	1 sprig parsley
Brussels sprouts	2 cups beef broth
½ cup water	¼ cup cream
1 small onion, sliced	1 egg yolk
pinch of marjoram	salt, pepper, and nutmeg

Cook the Brussels sprouts in water with onion, marjoram, and parsley until tender, about 10 minutes. Process in a blender or press through a wire strainer to make a purée. Add the beef broth and heat slowly. Beat cream and egg yolk together, and then slowly beat them into the Brussels sprouts purée (do not boil!). Taste; then season with salt, pepper, and a dash of nutmeg.

*FRENCH ONION SOUP

2 large onions, peeled and	2 slices French bread
sliced	2 slices Gruyère or brick or 2
3 tablespoons butter	tablespoons grated Parmesan
1 tablespoon flour	cheese
1½ cups canned beef broth	
(diluted according to label	
directions)	

Sauté the onions in the butter until golden and limp. Add the flour, blending to make a smooth paste. Slowly stir in the broth and bring to a boil. Boil for one minute.

Toast the bread. Lay a slice of cheese on each piece of toast. Pour the onion soup into two soup bowls. Top each with a slice of the toasted bread and cheese. If desired, slip the bowls of soup under the broiler for a few seconds to melt the cheese, but be sure to use heatproof bowls.

*SALMON SOUP

I like to keep a small can of salmon on hand so that, with onions and milk, I have the makings for Salmon Soup. This is an old "down on the farm" standby that I remember from childhood days.

8-ounce can salmon, bones and
  skin removed
2 cups milk
1 very thin slice onion

1 tablespoon butter
1 tablespoon flour
salt and pepper to taste
lemon juice to taste

Drain the salmon well. Heat the milk and onion to scalding (3 minutes). Remove onion, and discard. Melt the butter in a small pan, add flour, and gradually blend the hot milk into the mixture. Cook until thickened. Add the salmon; salt and pepper to taste. Squeeze in fresh lemon juice at the table, according to individual preference.

*VICHYSSOISE

After you try this out for two, try it on guests. You can serve it buffet-style with breads and cold cuts. Float a chunk of ice in it.

2 medium potatoes
1 small onion
2 tablespoons butter
3 cups chicken broth

¼ cup heavy cream
1 teaspoon chopped chives
dash of nutmeg
salt and pepper

Peel and cut up the potatoes. Slice the onion. Heat butter in a pan, add the onion, and cook gently and stir until onion is limp. Add the chicken broth and potatoes and boil gently, uncovered, until potatoes are tender. Put through a wire strainer, pressing the potatoes through, or process in a blender until smooth. Chill. Add the cream to the cold soup. Season with chives, nutmeg, salt, and pepper. If soup seems too thick, add more cream or chicken broth. Serve cold.

*TOMATO-POTATO SOUP

This soup can be made ahead and refrigerated until serving time. To serve, bring to the simmering point; add the cream and parsley last of all.

1 large tomato, peeled, diced
1½ cups water or chicken stock
1 medium-sized potato, peeled
1 small onion, chopped
1 tablespoon *each* butter and
    flour

salt and pepper to taste
⅓ cup heavy cream
parsley for garnish

In a 1-quart pan, combine the tomato, water or stock, potato, and onion. Bring to a boil, lower heat, and simmer until potato is tender (about 15 minutes). Process in a blender, or press through a wire sieve to make a purée. Melt the butter in the saucepan and add the flour. Slowly add the hot puréed mixture, stirring constantly. Cook until thickened and smooth, about 2 minutes. Taste; then add salt and pepper. Just before serving, stir in the cream and garnish with parsley.

*MOCK TURTLE SOUP

The "mock turtle" in mock turtle soup is veal or chicken meat.

2 tablespoons *each* butter and
    flour
2 cups canned beef broth
1 medium tomato, peeled and
    diced

1 tablespoon lemon juice
1 cup cooked, diced veal or
    white chicken meat
1 tablespoon cognac or Madeira

Melt the butter in a pan and stir in the flour. Add the beef broth, blending slowly until smooth. Heat to simmering; then add the tomato, lemon juice, and meat. Just before serving add the cognac or Madeira for flavor.

*PUMPKIN BISQUE

Ever wish you could find a use for a jack-o-lantern after Halloween is over? If the pumpkin is free from mold, cut it up and remove the skin. Simmer; then purée until smooth. The purée can be used in place of canned pumpkin in most recipes.

1 cup puréed pumpkin	2 thick slices French bread
1½ cups hot milk	salt and pepper to taste
4 teaspoons sugar	sour cream
	dash of nutmeg

Heat the pumpkin, milk, and sugar to simmering. Toast and butter the bread, and put a slice in each soup bowl. Pour the hot soup over the bread. Serve with salt and pepper, a bowl of sour cream, and a shaker of nutmeg—to be added at the table according to individual tastes.

*MEATBALL SOUP

Meatballs can be used in more than one kind of soup. This soup is low in calories but very flavorful.

2 cups canned beef broth	½ green pepper cut in
2 tablespoons instant minced	½-inch squares
onion or ¼ cup chopped	2 large mushrooms, quartered
whole green onion	pinch of basil
	½ pound lean ground beef
	soy sauce to taste

Heat the broth in a pan with the onion, green pepper, mushrooms, and basil. Shape the ground beef into 6 balls, and drop them into the simmering broth. Cover and simmer 15 minutes. Taste; then add soy sauce. Serve hot.

*MEATBALL PEA SOUP

Here's a different way to make split pea soup. Most recipes call for ham or ham hocks, but this one is based on ground beef.

½ pound (1 cup) green split peas (quick-cooking)	1 small carrot, peeled and diced
	¼ cup chopped onion
4 cups water	⅛ teaspoon ground allspice
¼ pound ground beef	salt and pepper to taste

Wash the peas well and add to the water in a 2- or 3-quart saucepan. Bring to a boil, lower heat, and simmer 45 minutes or until peas are soft. Shape the ground beef into small meatballs. Drop them into the simmering soup along with the carrot, onion, and allspice. Simmer about 1 hour longer. If the soup boils down considerably, add more water. Taste; then add salt and pepper. Serve soup hot with a pat of butter on top.

*CORN CHOWDER

1 small potato, peeled and diced	2 tablespoons water
1 small onion, quartered	8-ounce can whole kernel corn,
1 cup water	drained
½ teaspoon salt	1 cup milk
1 tablespoon flour	1 tablespoon butter
salt and pepper to taste	

Put the potato and onion in water; add the salt. Bring to a boil and cook 20 minutes, or until potato is tender. Mix the flour and 2 tablespoons of water, and slowly stir into the potatoes until blended. Cook until thickened. Add the corn, milk, and butter. Heat until soup just boils. Then remove and serve, adding salt and pepper to taste.

*QUICK SHRIMP BISQUE

This is great as a midnight or after-the-theater supper, or for lunch. Quick, too!

10-ounce can frozen cream of shrimp soup
½ cup milk

pinch of nutmeg
1 tablespoon sherry
dash of paprika

Thaw the soup and pour it into a pan. Add the milk, nutmeg, and sherry. Heat, stirring, until soup almost boils. Remove from heat and pour into serving bowls. Garnish with paprika.

*FRESH MUSHROOM SOUP

To make this soup you *must* use fresh mushrooms. Their flavor is unexcelled, whereas much of the flavor of the canned variety is long gone.

2 cups chicken broth (canned or homemade)
¼ cup finely diced celery
1 tablespoon instant onion, or 1 whole green onion, diced

¼ pound fresh mushrooms, sliced
salt and pepper to taste

Heat the broth and add the celery, onion, and mushrooms. Simmer 5 minutes, and serve. Add salt and freshly ground pepper to taste.

Eggs, Cheese, and Little Main Dishes

Eggs were probably the first convenience food known to man. They're neat and compact, and come in their own containers. They are also versatile, economical, high in food value, easy to prepare, and they combine with many flavors. So it seems odd that the commonest way to use them is fried, scrambled, boiled, or poached—for breakfast. We tend to forget some of the many variations for using eggs, which, nutritionally speaking, are a complete protein food and as adequate as meat in a meal. Here, along with basic cooking directions, are many interesting "little main dishes" using eggs.

Cheese, on the other hand, is one of the oldest man-made convenience foods and one of the most interesting to explore, when it comes to varieties. Each country, each ethnic group, has its own particular type of cheese—from the strongly flavored to the mild ones. Cheese with fruit is one of our favorite snacks. Exploring the combinations is great fun. Along with the classics like pears and provolone and apples and Cheddar, I find that grapes with Münster, and tangerines with cream cheese, are particularly pleasing.

Other little main dishes in this section, besides incorporating eggs and cheese, give you suggestions for using leftovers, and filling cream puffs and popovers in different ways.

Recipes that can be successfully doubled or tripled without further instruction are marked with an asterisk (*).

EGGS (*Basic Cooking Directions*)

There are two rules to remember. First, choose high-quality eggs, and then cook them at a moderate temperature. Grade A or AA eggs are best for boiling, poaching, or frying, but Grade B eggs are acceptable for scrambling or use in baked dishes.

"Boiling" eggs is really a misuse of the word. Eggs should not be boiled because that high a temperature makes the protein of the egg tough and leathery. A temperature of 185°, or just about simmering, is the best.

EGGS COOKED IN THE SHELL

There are two basic methods to choose from. The results vary a little, depending on the size of the eggs and the number you are cooking.

First Method: Cover eggs completely with cold water and bring water gradually to simmering. Do not let the water boil. Simmer 3 to 5 minutes for soft-cooked eggs. For hard-cooked eggs, simmer 15 to 20 minutes. Plunge eggs into cold water. They will shell easily if you tap them all over with the rounded side of a spoon and begin peeling from the large end. Hold the eggs under running water or dip them in water to help remove the shells.

Second Method: Cover eggs at least an inch with lukewarm water. Bring rapidly to the boiling point. Cover pan and remove from heat. For soft-cooked eggs, let stand 4 minutes. For hard-cooked eggs, let stand 15 minutes.

*BAKED OR SHIRRED EGGS

4 eggs   4 tablespoons milk or cream
                    salt and pepper

Butter two baking dishes or 10-ounce custard cups generously. Break two eggs into each, and add 2 tablespoons milk or cream to each dish. Sprinkle with salt and pepper. Place on baking sheet, cover, and bake at 325° for 20 minutes or until eggs are as firm as you like them.

Note: When baking eggs for more than two persons, you may wish to put all the eggs in one casserole. The eggs on the outer side of the casserole will cook more quickly than those in the center; this variation may work out well if either of you likes your eggs at different degrees of doneness.

BACON SHIRRED EGGS

Line the baking dishes with crisp crumbled cooked bacon before adding the eggs.

CHEESE SHIRRED EGGS

Line the buttered baking dishes with shredded cheese of your choice before adding the eggs.

FRENCH OMELET

4 eggs   ½ teaspoon salt
4 tablespoons water   butter

For best results, use an omelet pan 6 inches in diameter. Beat the eggs, water, and salt together with a fork. Heat the omelet pan until a drop of water sizzles, and butter it generously. Pour in the egg mixture all at once. Lower heat, lift up pan, and with a fork or spatula lift the omelet around the edges to allow uncooked mixture to run onto the bottom. Tilt and shake pan to keep the omelet loose from the pan. When the mixture no longer flows freely, the omelet is cooked. The omelet should *not* be browned, as this causes the egg to become overcooked and rubbery, and also results in an off-flavor. "Roll out," or fold, omelet onto a warm plate. Divide into two portions.

To serve four: Make 2 omelets.

To serve six: Make 3 omelets.

CHEESE OMELET

Make French Omelet and sprinkle the surface with ½ to ¾ cup shredded Cheddar, jack, or Swiss cheese before folding or rolling out onto a serving plate.

SPANISH OMELET

Make French Omelet and sprinkle the surface with ½ cup shredded jack or Cheddar cheese and 1 chopped peeled tomato. Add Tabasco sauce to taste before folding or rolling out onto warm serving plate.

MEXICAN OMELET

Make French Omelet and sprinkle the surface with ½ cup shredded jack cheese, 1 peeled and chopped tomato, and 1 chopped, canned green chili pepper before folding or rolling out onto a serving plate.

*CREAMY SCRAMBLED EGGS

4 to 6 eggs   ½ teaspoon salt
¼ cup cream   pepper to taste

Break the eggs into a bowl and beat with a fork until the yolks are broken. Add the cream and salt. Pour into the top of well-buttered double boiler or into a well-buttered frying pan set at low heat. Cook, stirring occasionally, until the mixture is set. Allow about 20 minutes for cooking, depending on the number of eggs used. Try to avoid cooking too quickly, as this makes the egg whites tough rather than creamy.

For a brunch party, scrambled eggs can be cooked over a hot-water bath in the chafing dish.

PUFFY RICE OMELET

2 eggs, separated
1½ teaspoons water
¼ teaspoon salt
½ cup cooked rice
2 tablespoons butter

1 tablespoon flour
½ cup milk
½ cup shredded sharp Cheddar
   cheese

Beat the egg yolks until thick and stir in the water, salt, and rice. Beat egg whites until stiff but not dry. Fold whites into the egg yolk and rice mixture. Melt half the butter in a 6-inch frying pan, and pour in the egg mixture. Cook over medium to low heat until golden brown on the bottom. Put into a moderately hot oven (350°) for 20 minutes or until the omelet is set.

Meanwhile, melt the remaining butter and blend in the flour. Stir in the milk, and cook until thickened and smooth. Add the cheese and stir until melted. Add salt and pepper to taste. To serve, turn the omelet out onto a hot platter, fold in half, and pour the hot cheese sauce over it.

To serve four: Double all quantities, making an omelet twice as big.

To serve six: Triple all quantities, but divide the mixture between two pans to bake (remember to butter them well), unless you have a very large frying pan that is ovenproof.

PUFFY OMELET

Your electric frypan is handy for this type of omelet.

4 eggs, separated
4 tablespoons water
½ teaspoon salt

butter
Tomato, Cheese, or Mushroom
   Sauce (see Index)

Put the egg whites into a bowl, add the water and salt, and beat until they are stiff. Beat the yolks thoroughly; then fold them into the whites. Heat butter in an 8-inch frying pan until a drop of water sizzles. Pour in the egg mixture, and cook over low heat until the bottom is set and very slightly golden. Cover and cook for 5 minutes or until set. Crease through the center, fold over, and roll onto a serving plate. Serve with your choice of sauce.

To serve four: Double the quantities and use a 10-inch frying pan.

To serve six: Triple the quantities and use a 12-inch frying pan, or simply make the basic omelet three times.

Alternate Method: Make the omelet as directed above except for the following. After the omelet is cooked on the bottom, finish cooking it by baking in a moderate oven (350°) for 10 to 15 minutes or until lightly golden. Serve the same as above, with Cheese, Tomato, or Mushroom Sauce.

POACHED EGGS ON TOAST

1½ quarts water	4 eggs
2 tablespoons vinegar or 1 table- spoon salt	buttered toast

Lightly grease a 2-quart saucepan, and add the water and vinegar or salt. Bring water to a gentle boil. Break the eggs into a saucer and slip them, one at a time, into the water. Reheat water to simmering; remove from heat and cover. Let stand 5 minutes or until eggs are as firm as you like them. Remove from water with a slotted spoon or slotted pancake turner. Slip 2 eggs onto a piece of buttered toast for each serving.

To serve four, six, or more: Simply cook 2 eggs per person, and serve as directed above.

POACHED EGGS ON SPINACH

Serve the poached eggs on cooked, buttered, well-drained spinach.

POACHED EGGS ON HASH

Serve the poached eggs on hot fried patties of corned beef hash.

POACHED EGGS ON HORSEBACK

Serve a poached egg on a cooked hamburger patty.

*POACHED EGGS IN PUFF NESTS

2 eggs
1 cup Béchamel Sauce (see Index)

½ cup shredded Swiss cheese
2 large Cream Puffs (see Index)

Poach and drain the eggs (see recipe for Poached Eggs on Toast for instructions). Make the sauce and add the cheese. Cut the top ⅓ off the cream puffs and insert a poached egg in each. Place cream puff tops over the eggs, and cover with sauce. Heat in a 450° oven for 5 minutes. Serve immediately.

Note: To serve as a hearty main dish rather than a luncheon-type serving, prepare two puffs per person.

*EGGS BENEDICT FOR TWO

Eggs Benedict in bed—what a luxury! But who's going to cook 'em?

2 poached eggs (see directions given earlier)
2 slices cooked ham

1 toasted English muffin, split and buttered
Hollandaise Sauce (see Index)

Poach the eggs until done to your liking. Meanwhile, heat the ham in a frying pan, and toast and butter the English muffin. Make the Hollandaise Sauce. To assemble, place a ham slice on each half of the muffin. Top ham with egg, and pour the Hollandaise Sauce over all.

Note: You may wish to make the Hollandaise Sauce ahead—or you may choose to serve Eggs Benedict when you have some Hollandaise left over. Simply reheat the sauce slowly over warm water, stirring, to keep it smooth. Heated too quickly, it will separate. If it should separate, process it in the blender to rehomogenize it (if you have a blender).

*EGGS MORNAY FOR TWO

Eggs Mornay make a beautiful luncheon or supper dish. Serve with toasted English muffins and coffee. Add fresh fruit for dessert. In the summertime, provide a whole platterful of fruit if serving a group.

3 eggs, hard cooked (see directions for Eggs Cooked in the Shell)

buttered, toasted English muffin

1 cup Mornay Sauce (see Index)

finely chopped parsley

Cook the eggs, remove shells, and cut eggs in half lengthwise. Place on toasted, buttered English muffin (3 egg halves per serving), and pour hot Mornay Sauce on top. Sprinkle with chopped parsley, and serve.

*EGGS WITH CRAB MORNAY

Prepare Eggs Mornay, but top the cooked eggs with 1 cup cooked crabmeat (½ cup on each serving) before adding the sauce.

SPINACH SOUFFLÉ

1 cup cooked spinach, chopped	2 egg yolks, slightly beaten
1 tablespoon butter	¼ cup shredded Swiss cheese
1 tablespoon flour	½ teaspoon salt
½ cup milk	dash of cayenne pepper
⅛ teaspoon salt	2 egg whites, beaten stiff

Drain the spinach well and press through a wire strainer or whirl in blender until puréed.

In a small pan heat the butter; add the flour, mixing until smooth. Blend in the milk and salt. Cook over medium heat, stirring, until thick and smooth. Remove from heat, and add the spinach, egg yolks, and cheese. Add salt and pepper. Fold in the egg whites. Pour into two well-buttered individual soufflé dishes, 1½ cup size, or into one small soufflé dish, 3 to 4 cup size. Bake in a moderately hot oven (375°) for 20 to 25 minutes or until soufflé is puffed and edges are tinged with a golden color. Serve immediately! This means *immediately,* for soufflés begin to fall as you take them out of the oven. It's best to have the guest ready and waiting at the table.

To serve four: Double all quantities and bake in individual soufflé dishes. If one large dish is used, it should hold 1 to 1½ quarts.

To serve six: Triple all quantities and make six individual soufflés; or use a large 2-quart soufflé dish and bake 15 minutes longer.

CHEESE SOUFFLÉ

It's far better to have your guests wait for the soufflé than to have the soufflé wait for the guests, for its high life is short but glorious.

2 tablespoons *each* butter and flour	1 cup shredded Cheddar cheese
1 cup milk	2 egg whites, beaten stiff
2 egg yolks	½ teaspoon salt and dash of pepper

Heat the butter in a pan, add the flour, and stir until well blended. Add the milk and cook until thickened and smooth. Cool to lukewarm, and stir in the egg yolks and cheese. Fold in the egg whites, and then add the salt and pepper. Pour into a buttered soufflé dish, about 2-cup size, or into two individual soufflé dishes each holding 1 to 1½ cups. (Fill dishes no more than ⅔ full.) If you have a dish that is only slightly too small, build up the sides with a collar made of foil.

Bake in a moderately hot oven (375°) for 20 to 25 minutes or until puffed and golden. Serve immediately.

To serve four: Double all quantities and use 1-quart soufflé dish or casserole.

To serve six: Triple all quantities and use a 1½-quart baking dish; use only 1 teaspoon salt, though.

*SCANDINAVIAN OVEN PANCAKE

For a brunch (late breakfast) or Sunday supper, here's an ideal dish. It goes wonderfully with a compote of fresh fruit.

1 strip bacon, cut into ½-inch pieces	1 egg, slightly beaten with ¾ cup milk
⅓ cup flour	⅓ cup whipping cream
2 teaspoons sugar	½ cup lingonberry preserves or canned cranberries
dash of salt	

For this pancake, use a frying pan that can go into the oven, about 5 to 6 inches in diameter. If you don't have one you'll have to transfer the pancake into an 8-inch pie pan.

Cook the bacon until it's crisp in a 5- or 6-inch frying pan or omelet pan. Don't pour off the drippings, but remove pan from the heat. Sift the flour, sugar, and salt into a bowl. Beat the egg lightly with milk, and stir into the dry ingredients; mix until smooth. Pour this batter over the crisp bacon and drippings in the frying pan. Bake in a moderately hot oven (375°) for 25 minutes or until set and lightly tinged with golden color. Meanwhile, whip the cream and blend it with the lingonberry preserves. Cut the pancake in wedges and serve with the lingonberry sauce.

*CHEESE ENCHILADAS

Tortillas are a round Mexican flatbread made of very fine corn-meal; check your grocery for them. Some stores keep them in the freezer cabinet; some have them canned. They're a fun thing to try when you're in an adventurous mood. Of course, if you live in the West, particularly the southern half of the West, tortillas are not news to you. My children call them "that bread that tastes like cardboard"—and that's supposed to be a compliment. They like tortillas!

Mexican-style red chile sauce usually comes in a can. It is made of red chile peppers, and should not be confused with Tabasco sauce, which is extremely hot, nor with the common chili sauce, which is quite sweet.

10½-ounce can Mexican-style red chile sauce

6 tortillas

2 hard-cooked eggs, chopped

½ pound shredded jack or Cheddar cheese of your choice (about 2 cups)

2 green onions, finely chopped

½ cup pitted ripe olives, sliced

Put the chile sauce into a large pan and simmer for 5 minutes. Dip each tortilla in the hot sauce and lay it on a plate. Spread a spoonful of hard-cooked egg across the center of each, along with some of the shredded cheese, chopped onion, and a few of the olives. Roll each tortilla up and lay, seamside down, in a baking dish. When all are rolled, pour any remaining sauce on top and add the remaining cheese and olives. Bake in a moderate oven (350°) for 15 minutes or until the sauce is bubbly.

*PUFFY CHILES RELLENOS

What a good combination this is! It's an almost authentic Mexican dish with quite authentic flavors. Serve it with Mexican hot sauce if you're so inclined. Serve also tortillas, refried beans, and cole slaw, and you're getting pretty Mexican!

3 eggs, separated
1½ teaspoons flour
⅛ teaspoon salt
dash of pepper

½ can (4-ounce size) whole
    green chiles
¼ pound mild Cheddar, brick,
    or jack cheese

Beat the egg whites until they are stiff, and set aside. Mix flour, salt, and pepper with the egg yolks; then fold the yolk mixture into the beaten egg whites. Pour *half* the resulting mixture into a greased baking dish the size of an 8-inch pie pan.

Wash 2 whole chiles and remove the seeds. Stuff the chiles with the cheese (cut in sticks); then place in the casserole on top of the egg mixture. Cover with the remaining egg mixture. Bake in a slow oven (325°) for 20 to 25 minutes or until puffy and tinged with gold.

CHEESE AND CORN HOT DISH

8-ounce can cream-style corn
½ cup soft bread crumbs
½ cup milk
½ small green pepper, chopped

½ teaspoon salt
dash of pepper
4-ounce package sliced Cheddar
    cheese

4 slices bacon

Combine the corn, crumbs, milk, green pepper, salt, and pepper. Pour into a greased baking dish, about ¾-quart size (a glass pie pan is about the right size). Lay the cheese slices over the top. Cook the bacon until crisp, and lay it over the cheese. Bake in a moderate oven (350°) for 15 to 20 minutes or until cheese melts and casserole bubbles around the edges.

To serve four: Double all quantities; use a 1-quart or 1½-quart casserole.

To serve six: Triple all quantities, using a 1½- to 2-quart casserole. Increase baking time to 30 to 35 minutes or until casserole is hot.

*FRENCH EGG CASSEROLE

Do you ever have extra hard-cooked eggs left over? At Easter-time, for instance? Here's a French egg casserole that tastes as if the eggs were cooked *just* for it. In fact, that's exactly what I do.

4 hard-cooked eggs	pinch each of thyme, marjoram,
4 slices bacon, cooked crisp	and basil
1 cup medium White Sauce (see	1 tablespoon chopped fresh
Index)	parsley
1 cup shredded sharp Cheddar	4 tablespoons buttered bread
cheese	crumbs
dash of garlic powder	

Peel the eggs and cut into thin slices. (Actually, you can use more eggs if you like, depending on how many you have on hand, but don't exceed 8 for this amount of sauce.)

Drain and crumble the bacon. Make the White Sauce, and add the cheese, garlic powder, thyme, marjoram, basil, and parsley to it. Pour a bit of the sauce into each of two individual casseroles, *au gratin* dishes, or 12-ounce custard cups. Add a layer of egg slices, then a few bacon crumbles, then more sauce. Continue layering until ingredients are used up, ending with the sauce. Sprinkle top with buttered bread crumbs. Bake in a moderate oven (350°) for 20 minutes or until bubbly around edges and crumbs are browned.

Note: To make buttered bread crumbs, heat 1 tablespoon butter until melted. Toss bread crumbs in the melted butter until evenly coated.

*CROQUE MONSIEUR

This fancy-sounding but classic sandwich is simply a ham and cheese sandwich cooked French toast-style. It's a good "quickie" to remember for a hasty lunch, Sunday supper, or midnight snack.

4 slices white bread (not that rubbery stuff, but homemade or good bakery bread)
butter (for spreading)
4 slices Gruyère or any favorite white cheese

2 slices ham
1 egg beaten with ¼ cup milk
butter for cooking
1 tablespoon salad oil

Spread bread with butter, and top two of the slices with a slice of cheese and a slice of ham, then another slice of cheese. Cover these with other two slices of buttered bread. Dip the sandwiches in the egg-milk mixture.

Heat about 3 additional tablespoons butter with the salad oil in a frying pan. Brown the sandwiches on both sides in butter, and serve hot (with sliced sweet pickle).

*SHRIMP-FILLED PUFFS or POPOVERS

½ pound fresh peeled shrimp (or frozen, uncooked)
1½ cups Béchamel Sauce (see Index)

1 teaspoon curry powder
dash of pepper
2 large cream puffs or popovers (see Index)

Rinse the shrimp and cook them in boiling salted water for 3 minutes or until they turn pink (don't overcook). Blend with the sauce, curry powder (adding more or less, to your taste), and pepper. Fill cream puffs or popovers and serve immediately.

*SAUSAGE PANCAKE

Instead of frying bacon first as in Scandinavian Oven Pancakes cook ¼ pound well-seasoned pork sausage until the pinkness is gone. Then proceed as directed in that recipe.

To serve four: Double all quantities.

To serve six: Triple all quantities and bake pancake in a 9-inch pan.

*CHEESE TARTS

Pastry for a single-crust pie (see Index, or use 1 cup or 1 stick
    pastry mix)

3-ounce package cream cheese
2 tablespoons milk
2 eggs
¾ cup shredded cheese—brick,
    Cheddar, or Gruyère
3 tablespoons butter

4 tablespoons flour
1½ cups milk
2 tablespoons tomato paste or
    catsup
¼ teaspoon salt
dash of cayenne pepper

Divide the pastry into two parts. Roll out each part and line
two individual-size *au gratin* dishes or pie pans about 4 to 6 inches
in diameter.

Soften the cream cheese and blend the 2 tablespoons of milk
in. Beat in the eggs until the mixture is smooth.

In a pan, heat the butter, add flour, blending well, and slowly
mix in the 1½ cups of milk. Cook and stir until the sauce is smooth
and thickened.

Blend the cooked sauce into the cream-cheese mixture; add the
tomato paste. Add salt and pepper to taste. Divide the mixture
between the pastry-lined pans and bake in a hot oven (400°) for
15 minutes. Lower heat to 300° and bake about 15 minutes longer,
or until filling is set.

STUFFED MAIN-DISH CREAM PUFFS or
    POPOVERS

Cream puffs and popovers are two items often overlooked for
quick and easy main-dish foods. I cannot understand why many
people say cream puffs are difficult to make. The procedure for the
dough resembles mixing up a packaged pudding; the shaping and
baking are similar to the process for drop cookies. For complete
directions, see the chapter "Breads and Basic Pastry."

Make a batch of cream puffs or popovers (see Index), and

freeze the extras. For a quick meal or for unexpected company, simply take the puffs out of the freezer and fill them. To thaw them quickly, place in a 350° oven for about 10 minutes. To fill the cream puffs, cut the top ⅓ off and spoon the filling in.

Some of the later recipes have fillings designed for cream puffs or popovers, and are given in amounts for just two people. Use them as basics, and remember the leftover possibilities they have.

*FRIED CHEESE SLICES

I found this idea in an old Hungarian cookbook—and if you are a cheese eater (I swear I'm a mouse!), you'll love these slices.

2 thick slices of a favorite cheese (sharp Cheddar, Gruyère, Swiss, etc.) about ⅓ inch thick

1 egg, slightly beaten
¼ cup dry bread crumbs
1 tablespoon butter for frying

Dip the cheese slices into egg, then into crumbs. Repeat until the egg is used up. Brown in hot butter over medium to high heat, turning over once. Serve immediately. Add a salad and bread sticks, and you're set for a balanced "little meal." But eat it hot!

*HAM-FILLED PUFFS

1 cup ground or finely diced ham
1½ cups Béchamel Sauce (see Index)
2 tablespoons chopped parsley

½ teaspoon tarragon
salt and pepper to taste
2 large cream puffs or popovers (see Index)

Combine the ham, Béchamel Sauce, parsley, and tarragon. Taste; then add salt and pepper. Fill cream puffs and heat for 5 minutes in a 450° oven to freshen the puff shells.

*RUSSIAN CHEESE PATTIES

We first tasted these fried cheese patties on a tourist trip to Leningrad. We had them for breakfast, along with sweet rolls and coffee.

1½ cups dry curd (uncreamed) cottage cheese	¼ teaspoon salt
	5 tablespoons flour
1 egg	butter for frying
1 teaspoon sugar	sour cream
	chives

Force the cheese through a fine sieve. Combine with the egg, sugar, and salt. Pinch off pieces of the dough and roll them into balls about the size of a golf ball. Roll lightly in flour; then press each ball into a patty about ⅜ inch thick. Brown quickly on both sides in hot melted butter. Serve with a topping of sour cream spooned on at the table. Garnish with chives if desired.

*MACARONI AND CHEESE

The numerous different shapes of macaroni on the market are fun to use in variety. In most recipes they can be used interchangeably; however, be sure to go by weight instead of measure, because some are bulkier than others. Check the package weight. Divide the contents of a 16-ounce package into two parts for an 8-ounce recipe—but in this case a "guesstimate" is really not too critical. Don't overcook macaroni and other pasta. Cook it *al dente* or so that it still has a bit of character left—so it is firm and chewy.

2 tablespoons *each* butter and flour	¼ cup shredded Cheddar cheese
	4 ounces elbow macaroni (about 1 cup)
¼ teaspoon salt	
1½ cups milk	¾ cup shredded Cheddar cheese

Melt the butter in a saucepan. Blend in the flour and salt. Gradually add the milk, stirring constantly; cook until sauce is thickened. Add the ¼ cup shredded cheese and stir until it is melted.

Cook the macaroni in boiling salted water as directed on the package, until tender. Drain. Add it to the cheese sauce and mix well. Turn into two individual baking dishes or casseroles, or into a 1-quart casserole. Sprinkle top with the remaining cheese, and bake in a moderately hot oven (375°) for 15 minutes or until cheese melts. Slip under the broiler and brown top of casserole.

BACON AND EGG QUICHE LORRAINE

pastry for a single-crust pie (see Index, or use 1 stick or 1 cup
    pastry mix)

¼ pound bacon	¾ cup cream or milk
2 eggs	½ teaspoon salt
	dash of cayenne pepper

Make the pastry and divide it into two parts. Roll out each part and line two individual-size (4-inch) pie pans with the pastry.

Cook the bacon until crisp, drain, and crumble into the pastry-lined pans. Beat the eggs, stir in the cream or milk, and add salt and pepper. Pour egg mixture over the bacon. Bake in a hot oven (400°) for 20 to 25 minutes or until filling is set in the center. Serve hot.

To serve four: Double all quantities and make four individual *quiches.* Or line a 9-inch pie pan with pastry for a single-crust pie; double filling ingredients, and pour into the pastry-lined pan. Bake at 400° for 15 minutes; lower heat to 350° and bake an additional 20 to 25 minutes or until pie is set in the center.

To serve six: Triple all ingredients and make six individual *quiches.* Or line a 10-inch round pie pan, or a square pan 9 by 9 by 2 inches deep, with pastry. Triple the filling ingredients and pour into the pastry-lined pan. Bake in a hot oven (400°) for 15 minutes; lower heat to 350° and bake an additional 25 to 30 minutes or until pie is set in the center.

*SWISS CHEESE FONDUE

This is one of the most romantic dishes to serve for two. Essentially, it is Swiss cheese melted in white wine. It's served in a fondue pot, and you dunk pieces of French bread into the mixture at the table. There are special cheese fondue pots on the market that consist of a heavy crockery-type pot set on a stand over an alcohol or Sterno burner, but you can improvise a substitute by using a heavy ovenproof casserole set over a can of Sterno. We have even prepared fondue on the range with the heat set at low, then transferred the pot onto a candle-warmer stand. Make absolutely sure to buy *imported* Swiss cheese. Domestic cheese is made with a different strain of bacteria, and it does not melt the same way. Don't heat the cheese too quickly or it may become stringy.

Another solution to making Cheese Fondue is to buy the already mixed that is packaged in Switzerland. It's excellent—and just the right amount for two. Only a crisp green salad is needed to complete the menu.

½ pound Switzerland Swiss cheese, shredded
1½ tablespoons flour
1 clove garlic
1 cup light, dry white wine (Rhine, Riesling, or Chablis)

salt, pepper, and nutmeg to taste
1 loaf French bread, cut into bite-size cubes

Dredge the cheese with flour. Rub the cooking utensil well with garlic. Pour in the wine, and set the pan over slow heat. When the wine is heated to the point where bubbles rise to the surface (not boiling), stir with a fork and add the cheese by handfuls, dissolving each handful completely before adding more. Keep stirring. When the cheese is all added and melted, add salt, pepper, and nutmeg to taste. Remove onto your table heating-element.

To serve, spear a piece of bread with a fork. Dunk it into the fondue pot in a stirring motion. Fondue should continue to bubble lightly.

CHEESE AND ONION QUICHE

pastry for a single crust pie (see Index, or use 1 stick or 1 cup pastry mix)

1 medium-sized onion	¾ cup cream or milk
1 tablespoon butter	1 cup shredded Swiss cheese
2 eggs	½ teaspoon salt
2 teaspoons flour	dash of pepper

Make the pastry and divide it into two parts. Roll out each part and line two individual (4-inch size) pie pans with the pastry.

Peel and chop the onion. Heat the butter in a pan. Add the onion and stir and sauté until golden. Remove from the heat. Beat the eggs; add the flour and cream. Blend in the cheese, salt, and pepper. Stir in the onions. Pour into the two pastry-lined pans. Bake in a hot oven (400°) for 25 to 30 minutes or until filling is set. Serve hot.

To serve four: Double all quantities. Make four individual *quiches,* or line a 9-inch pie pan with a single-crust pastry and double remaining ingredients; pour into pastry-lined pan and bake at 400° for 15 minutes; lower heat to 350° and bake an additional 20 to 25 minutes or until *quiche* is set in the center.

To serve six: Triple all quantities and make six individual *quiches.* To make a single large one for this number of people, you'll have to line a 10-inch round pie pan or a 9-inch square pan (2 inches deep). Triple filling ingredients and bake as directed for serving four; baking time will be longer by about 10 minutes.

*CHICKEN-FILLED PUFFS

1 cup cooked diced chicken
½ cup cream
1½ tablespoons lemon juice
½ cup finely minced celery

dash of paprika
dash of cayenne pepper
salt to taste
2 large cream puffs

Blend the chicken, cream, lemon juice, celery, paprika, and cayenne. Taste; then add salt. Spoon the mixture into the cream puffs and place on a cookie sheet. Heat in a 350° oven for 15 minutes or until the filling is heated through. Serve immediately.

Note: This is also a good way to use leftover cooked turkey, veal, or other roast; simply replace the chicken with whatever leftover roast you happen to have on hand.

*MUSHROOM-FILLED PUFFS

½ pound fresh mushrooms
2 tablespoons butter
½ cup cream

¼ cup shredded Swiss or
    Gruyère cheese
2 large cream puffs (see Index)

Wash and slice the mushrooms. Melt the butter in frying pan. Add mushrooms and cook for 2 to 3 minutes over high heat, stirring. Add the cream and cheese. Fill the cream puffs with the mixture. Put on a cookie sheet and crisp in a hot oven (450°) for 5 minutes. Serve immediately.

Note: These make tasty appetizers if the filling is put in very tiny cream puffs—about the size of a large walnut.

Fish and Shellfish

Did you know that about 240 species of fish and shellfish are marketed in the United States? No wonder that in the fish market so many different "names" are attached to the steaks, fillets, and whole fish. Fish recipes are pretty much interchangeable, though —if you keep in mind that fatty fish (like salmon) are best broiled or baked, and lean fish (like brook trout) do best under moist-heat cooking. But even this is not a hard-and-fast rule if you take care not to overcook fish. Overcooking produces a dry texture and strengthens an objectionable fishy flavor.

Aside from these restrictions, seafood possesses all the plus qualities for small-quantity cooking. It's easy to cook for just one or two because the pieces are usually small. It cooks quickly, and that's a real boon for quick meals. And the protein in fish and seafood is complete—equal to that in meats, poultry, and other animal products.

Happy fishing!

Recipes that can be doubled or tripled without further instructions are marked with an asterisk (*).

*COQUILLES SAINT-JACQUES

This makes two main-dish servings; however, if you're having guests, it is enough for 4 first-course servings.

1 tablespoon butter	½ pound scallops (fresh or
¼ cup dry white wine	frozen), quartered
1 teaspoon dried minced onion	½ cup heavy cream
¼ teaspoon salt	2 teaspoons lemon juice

¼ cup grated Parmesan cheese

In a pan, combine the butter, wine, onion, salt, and scallops. Bring to simmering and simmer for 3 minutes. Remove the scallops and arrange them in serving shells or individual serving dishes. Boil the remaining liquid until it is reduced to about ¼ cup. Add the cream and lemon juice, blend thoroughly, and boil until the sauce is thickened.

Pour the sauce over the scallops, dividing it equally between the two servings. Sprinkle with the Parmesan cheese. Broil about 5 inches below heat for 3 to 4 minutes or until browned and bubbling. Serve immediately.

*COQUILLES SAINT-JACQUES WITH MUSHROOMS

Make Coquilles Saint-Jacques as in the preceding recipe, and add ½ cup sliced, sautéed mushrooms to each serving. Then pour the sauce over, and proceed as above.

*POACHED SALMON, LAKE TROUT, or SWORDFISH STEAKS

2 fish steaks, 1 inch thick	½ cup white cooking wine or
	chicken bouillon

Béarnaise Sauce (see Index)

Put the fish steaks into a pan just large enough so that they will lie flat on the bottom. Pour in the wine or bouillon. Cover and simmer 8 to 10 minutes or until the fish flakes easily. Serve with Béarnaise Sauce.

*CRISP FRIED TROUT

2 rainbow trout or other small   dash of pepper
  fish, fresh or frozen   ¼ cup flour
  (thawed)   2 tablespoons yellow cornmeal
2 tablespoons milk   ½ teaspoon paprika
½ teaspoon salt   fat for frying

Clean the fish, wash, and wipe dry. Combine the milk, salt, and pepper. In another bowl combine the flour, cornmeal, and paprika. Dip fish in the milk mixture, then roll in the flour mixture. Deep-fry in hot fat (deep enough to cover the fish) for 4 to 5 minutes. (Fat should be about 375°.) Drain on paper toweling.

For four servings: Double all quantities.

For six servings: Triple the amount of trout, but just double remaining ingredients.

*TROUT AU BLEU

In order to make trout turn blue, they must be cleaned as soon as caught and cooked as soon as possible in acidulated water. Trout au Bleu is delightful when served with a Hollandaise Sauce, as suggested here.

2 fresh trout   4 tablespoons parsley
½ cup *each* water, white wine,   ¾ cup Hollandaise Sauce (see
  and vinegar   Index)

Clean trout as soon as possible after they are caught. Put them into a shallow pan, add the water, wine, and vinegar, and bring to simmering. Cook about 5 minutes or until the fish flakes when probed with a fork. Drain. Arrange on a serving dish, sprinkle with parsley, and serve hot with Hollandaise Sauce.

*TROUT LORRAINE

2 trout, about ½ pound each	¼ cup butter
2 tablespoons flour	salt
½ cup heavy cream	

Clean the trout but leave the heads on. Wash the fish well. Dry and roll in flour.

Heat half the butter in a frying pan and sauté the fish to brown on each side. Sprinkle with salt, cover, and cook 6 minutes. Arrange the trout on a hot serving dish or individual dishes and keep hot. Add the remaining butter and the cream to the frying pan. Heat but do not boil the mixture. Pour the sauce over the fish and serve immediately.

*BROOK TROUT AMANDINE

2 brook trout, cleaned	½ cup butter or oil
milk	¼ cup slivered or sliced almonds
flour	parsley
salt and pepper	lemon wedges

Dip the trout in milk, roll in flour, and sprinkle with salt and pepper. Heat the butter or oil in a frying pan. Add trout and cook until golden about 5 minutes on each side over moderate heat. Remove fish to a serving plate. Add the almonds to the pan drippings and heat through. Pour over the fish. Garnish with parsley and serve with lemon wedges.

*BROILED or BARBECUED FISH WITH
MAYONNAISE

1 pound fish fillets such as trout, lake trout, whitefish, cod	1 tablespoon lemon juice
	dash of cayenne
¼ cup mayonnaise	1 egg, separated

If you are barbecuing the fish, lay it on a long, narrow piece of foil to keep it from sticking to the grill. Barbecue or broil until the fish flakes easily.

Blend the mayonnaise, lemon juice, cayenne, and egg yolk. Beat the egg white until it is stiff. Mix the two parts together and spread mixture over the fish. Put under the broiler for 2 minutes or until lightly browned. Serve immediately.

CRACKED CRAB

Crab is cooked in much the same way as lobster, but generally it is bought already cooked. A large cracked crab weighing about 3 pounds is sufficient to serve two people. Bring it to the table on a bed of ice (if that's possible), or simply surround it with plenty of parsley for garnish. Provide lemon wedges and sauces such as Deviled Butter or Hot Mayonnaise to serve with the crab. Use a nutcracker to crack the legs and then pick out the meat. Dip it in sauce and eat. Only a green salad and hot French bread are needed to complete this delectable meal.

*LOBSTER THERMIDOR

2 lobster tails, about ½ pound each
2 tablespoons butter
2 teaspoons minced onion
dash of cayenne
3 tablespoons dry white table wine

¼ pound mushrooms, chopped
1 tablespoon tomato catsup
1 cup Béchamel Sauce (see Index)
2 tablespoons grated Parmesan cheese

Cook the lobster tails. Pick out and dice the meat; reserve the shells. Heat the butter in a pan. Add the onion, lobster meat, cayenne, wine, mushrooms, and catsup, and simmer 5 minutes. Blend in the hot Béchamel. Turn the mixture into the reserved shells. (It does not matter if it runs over slightly.) Sprinkle with Parmesan, and put under the broiler for 2 minutes or until lightly browned.

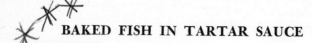

BAKED FISH IN TARTAR SAUCE

2 fish steaks, 1 inch thick   1 tablespoon chopped parsley
  (halibut, sea bass, salmon, or   1 tablespoon lemon juice
  lake trout)   ¼ teaspoon salt
1 cup sour cream   ¼ teaspoon *each* dry mustard
2 tablespoons *each* chopped   and basil
  green onion, green pepper,   dash of pepper
  and sweet pickle relish

Put the fish steaks into a greased baking pan. Combine the
remaining ingredients and pour over the fish. Bake in a 350° oven
for 30 minutes, or until fish flakes easily when probed with a
fork.

To serve four: Double all quantities.

To serve six: Triple the quantity of fish but just double the remaining quantities.

SOLE or PIKE FILLETS AMANDINE

3 tablespoons butter   salt and pepper
1 pound sole or pike fillets   ½ lemon
2 tablespoons flour   ½ cup sliced almonds

Melt the butter in a frying pan. Sprinkle the fish with flour, salt,
and pepper. Sauté in butter until golden on both sides. Squeeze
the lemon over. Put the almonds around the edges of the pan
and stir them until they are heated and lightly coated with butter.

To serve four: Double all quantities.

To serve six: Triple the amount of fish, but just double remaining
ingredients.

*BAKED SOLE WITH MUSHROOMS

4 fillets of sole (½ to ¾   2-ounce can chopped mush-
   pound)   rooms, including liquid
2 tablespoons dry white wine   2 teaspoons cornstarch
½ cup heavy cream   ¼ teaspoon salt

Arrange the sole fillets in a greased baking dish. Sprinkle them
with the white wine. Blend the cream, mushrooms, cornstarch, and
salt, and pour over the fish. Bake in 325° oven, basting frequently,
for 20 minutes or until fish flakes easily with a fork.

HAWAIIAN FILLET OF SOLE

2 large fillets of sole, pike, or   1 medium avocado, peeled,
   other mild-flavored fish   seeded, and sliced
salt and pepper   2 tablespoons chopped macada-
1 tablespoon lemon juice   mia nuts or blanched
flour   almonds
2 tablespoons butter   lemon wedges
¼ cup heavy cream

Sprinkle the fish with salt, pepper, and lemon juice. Let stand
10 minutes; then coat with flour. Heat the butter in a pan over
medium-high heat. Add the fish fillets, and brown on both sides.
Remove the fish. Add the cream to the pan and bring to a boil,
scraping pan to loosen the brownings. Spoon pan sauce over the
fish. Top with avocado slices and nuts. Serve immediately, with
additional lemon wedges.

To serve four: Double all quantities but cream, avocado, and nuts.

To serve six: Triple all quantities, but just double the cream, avocado, and nuts.

*TROUT IN CREAM

2 trout	¼ cup butter
salt and pepper	¼ cup white wine or apple cider
flour	¼ cup heavy cream

Clean the trout well, leaving the heads on. Gash on both sides from backbone to belly, 3 gashes on each side (this prevents curling). Sprinkle with salt and pepper and roll in flour. Heat the butter in a frying pan. Sauté trout 4 to 5 minutes on each side or until golden. Pour in the wine or cider and cook over low heat for 3 minutes more. Add the cream. Taste; then add salt and pepper. Cook until sauce is blended and slightly thickened.

*SOLE FLORENTINE

2 sole fillets (about ¾ pound)	2 tablespoons *each* water and butter
1 cup *each* water and dry white wine	1 cup Mornay Sauce (see Index)
10-ounce package chopped spinach or 1 pound fresh spinach	2 tablespoons grated Parmesan cheese

Put the fish into a small pan. Add the water and wine. Bring to the simmering point and cook about 5 minutes or until the fish flakes easily. Remove from heat. Drain. (Save liquid for use in sauces and soups calling for fish or chicken broth.)

Cook the spinach in butter and water until tender. (If using fresh spinach, wash it first very carefully to remove all the sand.) Lay cooked spinach in the bottom of a shallow broiler-proof serving dish or two individual dishes. Top with the fish. Pour the Mornay Sauce over evenly and sprinkle with grated cheese. Broil 1 minute or until lightly browned. Serve immediately.

*BROILED SALMON STEAKS

2 large fresh salmon steaks   1 tablespoon butter, melted
  (5 ounces each)   parsley for garnish
1 tablespoon oil   lemon for garnish
White Butter Sauce (see Index) salt and pepper to taste

Brush the salmon steaks with oil on all sides. Make the sauce. Brush the salmon with melted butter and broil about 4 inches from heat for 12 to 15 minutes, until they are browned on both sides, turning steaks once. Serve garnished with parsley and lemon. Add salt and pepper to taste and accompany with the White Butter Sauce in a bowl.

SOLE or PIKE FILLETS WITH MUSHROOMS

¼ pound fresh mushrooms,   ½ cup heavy cream
  sliced   1 teaspoon paprika
¼ cup butter   dash of salt
1 pound sole or pike fillets   2 tablespoons grated Parmesan
¼ cup dry white table wine   cheese

Sauté the mushrooms in half of the butter for 3 minutes. In another pan, heat the remaining butter, add the fish fillets, and sauté until golden on both sides. Transfer fillets to a serving dish. Add the wine to the pan and boil hard, scraping pan well, until entire amount is reduced to 1 tablespoon. Add the cream and boil until reduced to about half. Stir in the paprika. Add salt. Pour the mushrooms over the fish, and pour cream mixture over all. Sprinkle with Parmesan cheese and serve.

To serve four: Double all quantities.

To serve six: Triple all quantities, but be sure to use a pan with large bottom surface so that reducing the wine will not take so long.

*FISH FILLETS MOUSSELINE

½ cup Hollandaise Sauce (see
  Index)
4 tablespoons heavy cream,
  whipped
2 teaspoons lemon juice
2 large fish fillets (trout,
  salmon, or pike)

water, boiling
1 teaspoon salt
dash of pepper
parsley or watercress for
  garnish

Make the Hollandaise Sauce first. Combine it with the cream, add the lemon juice, and blend well. Keep warm until the fish fillets are cooked.

Place fillets in a frying pan and cover with boiling water. Add the salt and pepper, bring water to a boil, and simmer 3 to 4 minutes or until the fish flakes easily when probed with a fork. Remove fillets from the water, and arrange them on a warm serving dish. Spoon the sauce over the fish and garnish with the watercress or parsley. Serve immediately.

*SCALLOPS IN BUTTER

¾ pound scallops
¾ cup dry white cooking wine

¼ cup melted butter
1 tablespoon chopped parsley
paprika for garnish

Wash and drain the scallops (if scallops are frozen, thaw them under a stream of cool water). Put into a pan and add the wine. Bring to a boil, cover, reduce heat to medium or low, and simmer for 8 to 10 minutes. Remove scallops and slice each into 3 or 4 pieces. Arrange these in two individual *au gratin* dishes or on two scallop shells (you can buy them in gourmet cooking-utensil shops, even discount stores). Spoon 2 tablespoons of the melted butter over each serving, and sprinkle with parsley and paprika for garnish. Heat in a moderate oven (350°) for 5 minutes.

*SOLE or PIKE HOLLANDAISE

2 sole or pike fillets (¾ to 1
   pound)
salted water
¼ cup chopped parsley

2 medium potatoes, boiled,
   quartered while hot
4 tablespoons melted butter
Hollandaise Sauce (see Index)

Put the fish in a pan and cover with salted water. Simmer 10 minutes or until the fish flakes easily. Drain, arrange in serving dishes, sprinkle with parsley, surround with the potatoes, and pour the butter over the top. Serve with Hollandaise Sauce.

CRISP CRUSTED OYSTERS

2 tablespoons flour
dash of black pepper
¼ teaspoon ground allspice
16 large oysters (about 1
   pound), drained
1 egg, slightly beaten

⅓ cup fine dry bread crumbs
2 tablespoons finely chopped
   walnuts
2 tablespoons *each* butter and
   salad oil

Combine the flour with pepper and allspice. Roll the oysters in the mixture; let them dry for 15 minutes. Then roll in the beaten egg. Combine the bread crumbs and walnuts, and roll the oysters in this mixture. Let oysters stand another 15 minutes before cooking (this dries out the crust, which will become crisp while cooking). Heat the butter and oil in a frying pan. Add oysters and brown over medium-high heat about 4 minutes on each side. Serve hot.

For four servings: Double all quantities except the butter and oil; use 2 tablespoons of each as indicated above.

For six servings: Triple all quantities except the butter and oil; just double the amounts of those.

*OCEAN PERCH THERMIDOR

cooked perch fillets (about ¾
  pound)
2 tablespoons butter
2 tablespoons minced onion
dash of cayenne
3 tablespoons dry white wine
¼ pound mushrooms, chopped
  (about 1 cup)

1 tablespoon catsup
1 cup Béchamel Sauce or
  cream of mushroom soup
2 tablespoons grated Parmesan
  cheese

Dice the fish, removing the bones. Heat the butter in a pan, add the onion, cayenne, wine, mushrooms, and catsup. Simmer 5 minutes. Add the fish and heat through. Blend in the hot Béchamel Sauce, and turn the mixture into two scallop shells or onto two ovenproof serving dishes. Sprinkle with the Parmesan cheese and brown under the broiler for 1 to 2 minutes.

*SCALLOPS IN CHEESE SAUCE

¾ pound scallops
¾ cup dry white cooking wine
¼ pound white mushrooms,
  sliced
2 tablespoons butter
1 tablespoon flour

⅛ teaspoon salt
½ cup of the poaching liquid
¼ cup shredded Swiss or
  Gruyère cheese
1 cup mashed potatoes (can use
  mix)

1 tablespoon melted butter

Wash and drain the scallops (if they are frozen, thaw them under a stream of cool water). Put them into a pan and add the wine. Bring to a boil, cover, reduce heat to medium or low, and simmer 8 minutes. Remove scallops and reserve the liquid.

Sauté the sliced mushrooms in the butter for 4 minutes; remove from pan and divide between two individual serving dishes or scallop shells. Slice the scallops and layer them over the mushrooms in the serving dishes. Stir the flour into the pan drippings, add the salt and the reserved poaching liquid, and bring to a boil. Cook until it is thickened. Add the cheese. Divide the sauce between the two dishes, pouring it over the scallops.

Combine the potatoes with the melted butter and press through a decorating bag or spoon onto the edges of the individual dishes to make a decorative border. Brown in a moderately hot oven (375°) for about 8 minutes or until sauce begins to bubble.

*FISH FILLETS À L'ORANGE

¾ pound fresh or thawed frozen fish fillets (sole, ocean perch, or whitefish)
1 tablespoon melted shortening
1 tablespoon orange juice
1 teaspoon grated orange peel
½ teaspoon salt
dash *each* of nutmeg and pepper

Thaw frozen fillets. Cut into pieces 3 to 4 inches in size. Arrange these in a single layer, skin side down, in a well-greased baking dish. Combine remaining ingredients and pour over the fish. Bake in a moderate oven (350°) for 25 minutes or until the fish flakes easily when probed with a fork.

LOBSTER (*Basic Cooking Directions*)

Put the live lobster into a pot of boiling salted water (2 teaspoons salt to each quart of water). Slowly return water to a boil, and simmer it 15 to 20 minutes or until the lobster turns bright red. Remove pan from the heat and let the lobster cool in the liquid.

To remove the meat, crack the claws (use a nutcracker), separate the tail from the body, and pick out the meat. Discard the head sac, the dark vein, and lungs. Split the body also and take out the meat.

*SPANISH LOBSTER SALAD

1 cup cooked lobster
3 hard-cooked eggs
4 stuffed olives, chopped
2 teaspoons pickle relish or
   capers

⅓ cup mayonnaise
1 cup finely chopped celery
crisp lettuce

Cut the lobster into small pieces. Chop the eggs and add to the lobster along with the olives, relish, mayonnaise, and celery. Chill. Serve over crisp lettuce.

*LOBSTER NEWBURG

1 cup diced cooked lobster
2 tablespoons butter
2 tablespoons flour
1 cup light cream

salt and pepper to taste
dash of paprika
dash of Tabasco
1 tablespoon sherry

Melt the butter in a pan and add the flour; stir in the cream and cook slowly (don't boil) until thickened. Add salt and pepper to taste, and blend in the lobster, paprika, Tabasco, and sherry. Serve over hot toast points or in patty shells.

*LOBSTER SHERRY

4 lobster tails (small, frozen)
boiling salted water
3 tablespoons butter
4 tablespoons sherry
pinch of cayenne

2 egg yolks
⅓ cup heavy cream
¼ cup sour cream
2 egg whites (whipped)
dash of salt

Cook the lobster as directed on the package, in boiling salted water. Remove the meat from the shells and cut it up. (Reserve the shells.)

Melt the butter in a pan. Blend in the sherry, cayenne, egg yolks, and cream. Cook and stir over low heat until thickened. Taste; then add salt.

Put the cut-up lobster back into the shells. (If shells were destroyed, use scallop shells or small casseroles.) Pour the sauce on top. Sprinkle with parsley; then top with whipped egg whites. Broil until lightly browned, about 4 inches from the heat.

*SEAFOOD PICNIC SALAD

1 cup cleaned, cooked shrimp, crab, or diced lobster	2 tablespoons fresh lemon juice
½ cup chopped raw cauliflower	1 tablespoon French dressing
1 tablespoon chopped stuffed green olives	¼ cup mayonnaise
2 tablespoons finely minced green pepper	1 teaspoon finely minced mild onion
	lettuce

Combine the seafood with the cauliflower, olives, and green pepper. Chill. Blend the lemon juice, French dressing, mayonnaise, and onion, and pour over the shrimp mixture. Toss well. Serve in bowl lined with lettuce.

*SEAFOOD SCRAMBLE

2 tablespoons butter	1 cup cooked crabmeat, sliced lobster, or shrimp, or a combination
5 eggs	
1 tablespoon cream	
2 tablespoons sherry	¼ cup cooked tiny shrimp
¼ teaspoon salt	2 tablespoons sliced almonds

Heat the butter in a frying pan over high heat. Blend the eggs, cream, sherry, and salt, and pour the mixture into the hot butter. Stir gently as the eggs begin to set. Add seafood and almonds when the eggs are about half done. Cook until done to your liking. Serve.

*PORTUGUESE-STYLE LOBSTER

2 cups diced cooked lobster | 1 cup tomato sauce
1 small onion, chopped | 1 tablespoon flour
2 tablespoons butter | 2 tablespoons brandy or 1
½ teaspoon salt | tablespoon lemon juice
dash of pepper | 2 cloves garlic, mashed

Fluffy Rice (see Index)

Put the diced lobster into a heatproof dish.

In a separate pan, sauté the onion in butter until golden. Add the salt, pepper, and tomato sauce. Sprinkle in the flour. Add the brandy and garlic, and simmer 5 minutes. Pour this sauce over the lobster. Heat to serving temperature. Serve with hot Fluffy Rice.

*CRAB-FILLED MUSHROOMS

4 large mushrooms (3 or 4 | 3 tablespoons sherry (optional)
   inches in diameter) | ½ teaspoon tarragon
salted water | 1 cup cooked crabmeat
2 tablespoons butter | 1 teaspoon cornstarch
½ cup heavy cream | ½ cup diced mild white cheese

Wash the mushrooms. Remove stems from caps, and put caps in salted boiling water. Boil 3 minutes and drain.

Chop the stems. Heat the butter in a pan, add the chopped stems, and sauté 3 minutes. Add the cream, sherry, and tarragon to the pan and boil fiercely, stirring, until the liquid is reduced to about half. Blend the crabmeat and cornstarch, and add to the cream mixture in the pan. Simmer 5 minutes.

Put mushroom caps on a heatproof serving dish. Fill them with the cream mixture, top with the diced cheese, and broil until cheese melts. Serve hot.

FROGS' LEGS PROVENÇALE

Because it is not always easy to find cooking directions for such things as frog legs, the recipe is included here. In fact, sometimes it is fun just to read such recipes. But this recipe also prompts tasting because, prepared this way, frog legs are very good indeed. You can buy frog legs frozen (best to telephone around before you embark on a shopping trip—you'll save many steps). Or you may be lucky enough to have wild ones available. Skin the legs, trim off feet, and the legs are ready for cooking. How many to allow per serving depends on their size. If they are small, 6 or 8 may be necessary, but with large ones, 1 or 2 may be enough. (If the frog legs you buy are saddles, simply cut them apart to make individual legs.)

½ to ¾ pound frogs' legs
milk
seasoned flour (1 cup flour, 1
   teaspoon salt, ¼ teaspoon
   pepper)

½ cup each olive oil and butter
1 clove garlic, finely minced
2 tablespoons finely minced
   parsley

Soak the frogs' legs in milk to cover for 2 hours (in refrigerator). Dip them in the seasoned flour; then shake off surplus, and allow to dry for a few minutes. Heat the olive oil, butter, and garlic in a frying pan or heavy saucepan. Add the frogs' legs and sauté on all sides until they are golden. Small ones should cook about 4 to 5 minutes, large ones about 10 minutes. If overcooked, they are tough. Serve garnished with parsley.

To serve four: Double all quantities except garlic; use only 1 clove.

To serve six: Triple all quantities except oil, butter, and garlic. Use 1 cup each oil and butter and 1 clove garlic.

*CRAB NEWBURG

¼ pound cooked crabmeat   1 tablespoon sherry
2 tablespoons butter   1 egg yolk
dash of salt   ½ cup cream
dash of cayenne   toasted croutons or toast points

Heat the crab in the butter. Add salt, cayenne, and sherry. Beat the egg yolk and cream together, and add to the crab. Cook, stirring carefully, but do not boil. Serve in scallop shells topped with croutons, or serve over toast points.

*SHRIMP NEWBURG

Make Shrimp Newburg with the recipe for Crab Newburg, using cooked shrimp instead of the crabmeat.

*PEPPERED SHRIMP AND EGGS

¼ pound cooked, peeled,   ¼ teaspoon salt
   cleaned shrimp   dash of cayenne pepper
1 slice bacon   2 eggs, beaten
¼ cup chopped green pepper   2 tablespoons light cream
¼ cup chopped onion   dash of Worcestershire sauce

If the shrimp are frozen, thaw them; then cook and drain.

Fry the bacon until crisp; drain and crumble it, and set aside until later. Cook the pepper and onion in the bacon fat until tender. Add salt, pepper, and the shrimp. Heat through.

Combine the reserved bacon with the beaten eggs, the cream, and Worcestershire sauce. Add to the shrimp mixture, and cook until the eggs are set but not dry, stirring occasionally.

*SOUR CREAM SHRIMP SALAD

1 cup cooked chilled shrimp
shredded crisp lettuce
½ cup sour cream

1 tablespoon lemon juice
salt and pepper to taste
lemon wedges

Arrange the shrimp over shredded lettuce and chill well. Mix the sour cream, lemon juice, salt, and pepper, and spoon over the shrimp. Serve with lemon wedges.

OYSTERS À LA KING

½ pint fresh oysters
melted butter
1 cup medium White Sauce
   (see Index)
1 tablespoon sherry

¼ teaspoon curry powder
pinch of powdered saffron
shredded lettuce
2 slices buttered toast, quartered
chives and parsley for garnish

Wash and drain the oysters. Place them on a piece of foil on a baking pan, brush with melted butter, and broil for 5 minutes about 5 inches from the source of heat. Watch carefully.

Combine the White Sauce, sherry, curry powder, and saffron. Line serving plates with lettuce. Top lettuce with the broiled oysters. Pour the seasoned White Sauce on top, surround with toast quarters, garnish with chives and parsley, and serve.

For four servings: Double all quantities.

For six servings: Triple all quantities except seasonings. Double seasonings, taste, and add more if needed.

*POACHED OYSTER SALAD

8-ounce can whole oysters,
   drained (or 1 cup fresh
   oysters poached in 1 cup
   water for 5 minutes)
crisp lettuce

1 tablespoon white wine vinegar
¼ cup mayonnaise
lemon wedges and parsley for
   garnish

Arrange the oysters on lettuce (for 2 individual servings). Blend vinegar and mayonnaise and spoon over each serving. Chill. Garnish with lemon wedges and a sprig of parsley.

Meats

Meats to cook for two may seem like a problem. Yet portion cuts are some of the best for variety, and there are many to choose from. Cooking meat for two can be especially exciting because you can buy just two pieces of a deluxe cut, prepare a gourmet meal, and spend much less than you would if you were eating out.

We give a variety of ways to serve everything from lamb chops to ground beef patties. Try them all, and use your imagination to invent new ways to serve your favorites. Use the recipes as a guide, but don't be limited by them. If garlic disagrees with you—or onion—or some other ingredient—don't use it. Most of the recipes will not be spoiled by the omission of this type of ingredient, but do use your own good judgment in correcting the seasoning so that the dish tastes balanced. Often, only the amount of salt and pepper needs adjustment.

Recipes that can be doubled or tripled without further instruction are marked with an asterisk (*).

TIED BEEF—RARE SIRLOIN

¾ pound sirloin roast, well tied   5 cups bouillon
                                5 cloves garlic

Have butcher tie the roast well. Bring bouillon and garlic to a
boil. Add meat, return to a fierce boil, and boil it hard for 8 to 10
minutes. Remove from broth and cut into thin slices. Serve with
Béarnaise, Anchovy, or Horseradish—Sour Cream Sauce. The meat
will be (and must be) very rare to be good. Excellent for open
sandwiches!

To serve four: Cook two roasts, ¾ pound each (not a double-size
one).

To serve six: Cook two roasts, about 1 pound each.

STANDING RIB FOR TWO

The flavor of a juicy rib roast is here, though you need buy only
one rib. The roasting time will vary; I've given the "average"
here. A rib from the small end of the loin is thicker and requires
more time. The only sure gauge is to use a meat thermometer.

1 rib of standing rib roast,   ½ teaspoon seasoned pepper
   about 2 pounds   (optional)
1 tablespoon butter   ½ teaspoon salt
1 clove garlic, mashed

Buy just one rib of a standing rib roast; do not let the butcher
break the bone. Combine butter, garlic, seasoned pepper, and salt.
Rub meat with the butter mixture. Wrap well and freeze until
solid. (You can do this ahead and have the roast ready to slip into
the oven about 1½ hours before you plan to eat.)

Remove meat from freezer and unwrap, being careful not to
remove the butter mixture. Stand it on a baking sheet (a piece of
crumpled foil on either end of the bone helps to keep rib up-

right). Scrub two baking potatoes, rub lightly with oil, and place on the pan with the meat. Roast in a hot oven (400°) for 1¼ hours for rare meat, 1½ hours for medium-rare, or 1¾ hours for well-done meat. To check for doneness, use a meat thermometer. Simply insert it down the center of the meat, and wait a few seconds for it to register. Because of the variation in one-rib cuts, this is the surest way to tell whether the meat is done to your liking. Let roast stand 5 minutes before carving. To serve, simply cut entire roast into two slabs of meat.

To serve four or six: Buy two ribs of standing rib roast; wrap and freeze in the same manner. After one hour of cooking, insert meat thermometer, and cook until desired degree of doneness is reached. Use same amount of seasoning and same degree of heat as for a single rib.

*WINE-MARINATED PICNIC BURGERS

Shape hamburger into patties, separate with plastic wrap, and stack in a container, ready for cooking at the picnic site. (You can freeze them if you plan to use them for picnic lunches while traveling.)

¾ pound lean ground beef   ¼ cup dry red cooking wine
                    dash of garlic powder

Shape the ground beef into two thick patties. Combine the wine and garlic powder. Stack patties in picnic container (plastic refrigerator containers work fine), with a folded piece of waxed paper between them. Pour the wine marinade over the patties. Refrigerate or keep cold until ready to cook.

Note: We've stacked several hamburgers in a 2-quart milk carton, poured a marinade over, and frozen the whole lot; then we cooked them as needed while traveling or camping. Even if the patties are frozen the first night, you can thaw-cook them over a barbecue fire or in frying pan over your camp stove.

FONDUE BOURGUIGNONNE

Beef fondue is great to serve when you want a slow and leisurely meal. Take the meat to the table raw, spear meat cubes with a wooden-handled fork, and cook each piece of meat to your liking in the fondue pot of hot oil.

¾ pound beef tenderloin or
 sirloin steak
1 cup butter (½ pound)
1 cup olive oil or salad oil

choice of (see Index):
 Rémoulade Sauce
 Tomato Sauce
 Béarnaise Sauce
 Curry Sauce
 Sweet and Sour Sauce

Cut beef into ¾-inch cubes. Melt butter in a beef fondue pot or in the top of a chafing dish over direct heat. Add the oil and bring to a boil (this is done at the table). Spear cubes of meat and hold them in the hot butter-oil mixture until meat is done to taste. Spoon sauce over meat and eat with a slice of crusty French bread.

To serve four: Double amount of meat but not of butter and oil.

To serve six: Triple the amount of meat but not of butter and oil.

Note: After using, cool the cooking oil and strain it into a freezer container to save for another Fondue Bourguignonne.

GOURMET CHATEAUBRIAND

This is "ah-elegant," and worth any painstaking preparation it may take.

½ cup dry white wine
1 tablespoon minced shallots or
 green onion (bulb part)
2 tablespoons *glace de viande*
 (see below)
1 tablespoon butter

1 teaspoon lemon juice
½ teaspoon crushed tarragon
1-pound Chateaubriand steak
 (cut from thickest part of
 tenderloin)
butter

Combine wine and shallots in pan. Bring to a boil over high heat, and boil 5 minutes or until liquid is reduced to about half. Add the *glace de viande,* butter, lemon juice, and tarragon. (Make the *glace de viande* ahead but keep it in a jar in the refrigerator; use it also to enrich soups, sauces, stews.)

Broil the steak about 3 inches from the heat until it is done to your liking, spreading it with butter to keep it from drying under the broiler. Pour hot sauce over steak when ready to serve. Slice to serve at table.

Glace de viande: Boil a 10½-ounce can of beef bouillon until it is thick and reduced to about ½ cup.

POT AU FEU

Serve this French stew over rounds of toasted French bread in individual soup plates.

1 pound lean beef, cut in 1-inch cubes	1 stalk celery, cut in 2-inch pieces
1 teaspoon salt	½ small turnip, peeled and cubed
cold water	1 sprig parsley
1 small onion, chopped	½ small bay leaf
1 whole clove	1 clove of garlic
1 carrot, peeled and halved	

Put the beef and salt into a saucepan. Cover with water. Add the onion, clove, carrot, celery, turnip, parsley, bay leaf, and garlic. Bring to a boil. Reduce heat, skim off brownish foam, and cover. Simmer 2 hours or until beef is very tender. Strain broth. Return broth to meat. Serve over hot toasted French bread rounds.

To serve four: Double all quantities, but use only 1 clove of garlic.

To serve six: Triple all quantities but use only 1 large clove of garlic.

*BEEF BROCHETTES

½ pound boneless sirloin steak
3 slices bacon
2 to 3 tablespoons melted butter
salt and pepper to taste

Cut meat into 1-inch cubes. Cut bacon into squares. Alternate meat and bacon on two skewers, dividing the amounts equally. Paint with melted butter. Broil 3 inches from heat or over hot charcoal, turning to brown on all sides, until meat is done to your liking.

FLANK STEAK BROIL

1 small flank steak, about 1 pound
¼ cup *each* soy sauce and sherry
2 tablespoons honey
2 tablespoons finely chopped preserved ginger
1 clove garlic, mashed

Trim the steak and lay it in a shallow pan (such as a cake pan). Combine remaining ingredients and pour over. Marinate 8 hours. Drain and reserve marinade; it can be used again on hamburgers and chicken.

Broil steak over hot coals, or in a very hot frying pan, for 3 to 5 minutes on one side. Turn over and spoon on 2 to 3 tablespoons of the marinade. Cover pan and cook for 8 minutes. If you're using charcoal, broil the steak for 8 minutes on each side; it should be quite rare. To serve, cut very thin slices (⅛ to 1/16 inch thick) across the grain. If you slice diagonally rather than straight up and down, you'll have wider slices.

To serve four: Choose a large flank steak—2 pounds or more. Use same amount of marinade as above.

To serve six: Cook 2 flank steaks about 1½ to 1¾ pounds each, and double the marinade amounts.

*LONDON BROIL TERIYAKI

1 pound (2 pieces) rolled flank   Teriyaki Marinade (see below)
  steak prepared for London
  broil, skewered

Meat markets often feature a rolled and sliced cut of beef flank steak labeled "London Broil." Each slice is skewered together in a roll that measures about 4 inches in diameter; it is about 1 inch thick. Usually the cut is across the grain of the flank, and often the flank has been run through a tenderizer before it is rolled, sliced, and skewered. To prepare teriyaki-style, marinate in Teriyaki Marinade for 3 to 4 hours or longer. Barbecue, grill, or broil until done to your liking (5 minutes on each side for rare). Serve as you would a steak.

Teriyaki Marinade: Combine 3 tablespoons imported soy sauce, 1 tablespoon salad oil, 2 teaspoons honey, 2 teaspoons sherry, 1 small clove garlic (crushed), and 1 teaspoon grated fresh ginger *or* ¼ teaspoon powdered dry ginger. Mix well.

GOURMET STEAK

1 club steak, 2 inches thick   salt and pepper (freshly
½ cup cognac or brandy   ground)

Gash fat edge of steak at ½-inch intervals to prevent curling. Marinate in the cognac or brandy for 30 minutes. Then broil over hot charcoal until done to your liking—about 14 to 20 minutes (total time) for rare; 20 to 30 minutes for medium rare; 30 to 35 minutes for medium, and 45 minutes for well done. Season with salt and freshly ground pepper.

To serve four to six: Marinate a 5-pound sirloin steak (about 2 inches thick) in 1 cup cognac or brandy, and cook as directed.

PLANKED STEAK

2 steaks, T-bone or club,   oil
  1½ inches thick   Spiced Potatoes (see Index)
garlic   or French fried potatoes
butter   salt and freshly ground pepper

Rub steaks on both sides with a cut clove of garlic, and coat one side of each with melted butter. Broil for 5 minutes (for rare steak).

Rub a hardwood cooking plank with oil. Cover the edges and exposed portions of the plank with foil to prevent burning it. Lay steak, broiled side down, on the plank. Surround with Spiced Potatoes and broil about 4 inches from source of heat for another 5 minutes for rare meat, or 8 to 10 minutes for medium-rare steak. If you plan to cook medium-rare steak, do not add the potatoes until the meat has cooked half the time, or they will get too brown. Season with salt and pepper.

To serve four to six: Choose a thick steak weighing 3 to 4½ pounds, and carve into individual servings at the table.

Note: Use a hardwood plank 1½ to 2 inches thick. You can buy a suitable piece from most lumberyards. Be sure it is sanded smooth; then treat it with salad oil before using. Also be sure to keep the wood moist, or cover the edges with foil, while cooking so that it will not scorch. After each of the first few uses, wash the plank in warm water, dry, and re-treat with oil.

*STEAK WITH BLUE CHEESE

2 individual-size steaks (club,   2 tablespoons butter
  T-bone, sirloin, or   2 tablespoons blue cheese
  tenderloin)   salt and pepper

Broil steaks about 3 inches from heat, allowing 3 to 6 minutes on each side. Mash together the butter and blue cheese with a fork. Put steaks on hot individual serving dishes. Sprinkle with salt and grind pepper over top. Dab each steak with half of the cheese mixture. Serve immediately.

*HUNGARIAN BEEF GOULASH

1 tablespoon bacon drippings or salad oil
1 pound lean beef stewing meat
1 cup water
2 onions, coarsely chopped
¾ teaspoon paprika
¾ teaspoon salt
½ green pepper, coarsely chopped

Heat drippings in a heavy frying pan. Add beef and brown well. Add water and stir to loosen brownings from the bottom of the pan. Cover and simmer for 1½ to 2 hours or until meat is very tender. Add more water if necessary to keep meat moist. Add the onions, paprika, salt, and green pepper, and simmer 15 minutes more.

*BEEF BURGUNDY AND BRAISED VEGETABLES

1 tablespoon butter
¾ pound lean stewing meat
1 tablespoon flour
¼ teaspoon *each* salt and pepper
¾ cup red cooking wine
1 small clove garlic
¼ teaspoon *each* dried parsley and thyme
½ small bay leaf
2 small onions, quartered
2 carrots, peeled and sliced
4 fresh mushrooms, whole

Melt butter, add beef, and brown about 10 minutes on medium-high heat. Add flour, salt, pepper, wine, garlic, parsley, thyme, and bay leaf. Simmer 2 hours or until meat is tender. Add the onions, carrots, and mushrooms, and simmer ½ hour more.

*BEEF AND MUSHROOMS VINAIGRETTE

An excellent main dish to make ahead; leave it in the refrigerator until serving time.

¼ pound fresh mushrooms,
  sliced
2 teaspoons olive oil or salad oil
1 tablespoon lemon juice
1½ teaspoons chicken stock
  base
½ pound leftover beef roast, cut
  in strips (about 2 cups)

1½ teaspoons red wine vinegar
2 tablespoons red cooking wine
1½ teaspoons oil
1 tablespoon chopped parsley
½ teaspoon *each* crumbled chervil and tarragon
⅛ teaspoon dry mustard
salt to taste

½ Bermuda onion, thinly sliced

Sauté the mushrooms in the oil. Add the lemon juice and chicken stock base (or use 1 chicken bouillon cube). Cover and simmer 5 minutes. Add the beef, vinegar, wine, oil, parsley, chervil, tarragon, mustard, and salt to taste. Add the onion, remove from heat, cool, cover, and chill for 3 hours. Serve with shredded lettuce.

*SLICED BEEF AU CRÈME

1 pound beef rump sliced about
  ¼ inch thick
2 tablespoons butter
6 anchovy fillets, chopped
⅓ cup parsley, chopped
2 tablespoons chopped sweet
  onion
1 stalk celery, chopped
1 small carrot, chopped

½ teaspoon coarse ground
  pepper, or freshly ground
  pepper
½ teaspoon fennel
2 tablespoons Madeira or sherry
¼ cup beef bouillon (about)
1 cup heated heavy cream
2 tablespoons brandy or cognac
1½ teaspoons paprika

parsley for garnish

Brown the beef quickly in the butter in a frying pan over high heat; remove from pan, reserving pan and juices.

Lay a slice of the beef in the bottom of a buttered, heavy casserole that can be used for top-of-stove cooking. Sprinkle with a little of the anchovy, parsley, onion, celery, carrot, pepper, and fennel. Stack remaining slices over first one, sprinkling each in the same manner with the vegetables and seasonings.

To the juices in the frying pan, add the Madeira and beef bouillon, bring to a boil, and cook for 2 minutes. Pour this over the meat in the casserole. Then pour the hot cream over the meat. Cover and cook over very low heat for about 1 hour or until tender, adding more bouillon if necessary to keep meat almost covered with liquid.

Remove meat to a heated platter. Heat the brandy or cognac, ignite, and pour over the meat, flaming. Strain the sauce in the casserole and cook until it is slightly reduced and thickened. Stir in $1\frac{1}{2}$ teaspoons paprika and cook 1 minute. Pour over the meat; garnish with more chopped parsley.

*VEAL SCALLOPINE

¾ pound veal round steak	¼ cup butter
salt and pepper	⅓ cup dry white table wine
flour	salt and pepper to taste

Cut the round steak into individual "muscles" or into approximately 3-inch squares. Put a piece between two sheets of waxed paper. With the flat side of a meat mallet, or with a wooden mallet or rolling pin, pound meat until it is very thin and about doubled in length and width. Repeat for each piece of meat.

Sprinkle meat with salt, pepper, and flour. Heat butter in frying pan, and cook the meat quickly on both sides until it is light golden in color. Remove meat from pan, stir in the wine, and boil hard until liquid is reduced to about 4 tablespoons. Pour juices over the meat and serve, adding salt and pepper to taste.

RIB EYE WITH MUSHROOMS

1 boneless rib steak, ¾ to 1   ¼ pound fresh mushrooms,
  pound   sliced
4 slices bacon, cut in ½-inch   4 tablespoons butter
  pieces   ½ cup dry white table wine
             salt and pepper to taste

Gash fatty edge of steak at 1½-inch intervals so that it will not curl while cooking. Cook bacon until crisp in large frying pan; remove and drain all but 1 tablespoon of bacon fat. Add the mushrooms and butter to pan. Get pan very hot, push mushrooms to one side, and put steak into pan. Sear on one side and turn over. Cook about 4 minutes on each side for medium-rare meat. Transfer steak to a heated platter. Arrange bacon on one side of steak. Spoon mushrooms onto other side. Add wine to pan and scrape to release brownings. Boil about 2 minutes and pour this sauce over the meat.

To serve four: Double all quantities; however, brown the mushrooms and remove them from pan (keep hot) before cooking steaks, or pan will not hold all the meat.

To serve six: Triple all quantities, following the same advice.

*BEEF STROGANOFF

¾ pound sirloin steak   salt, pepper, paprika
2 tablespoons butter   2 shallots or green onions
        ½ cup commercial sour cream

Cut meat into ½-inch slices about 2 inches wide. Heat butter in frying pan; then sauté meat in butter for 5 minutes. Sprinkle with salt, pepper, and paprika. Chop the shallots or green onion fine, and add to the pan. Cook until shallots are tender. Stir in the sour cream, and heat without boiling to serving temperature. Serve at once.

*FRENCH PEPPER STEAK

2 boneless rib steaks	⅓ cup water
1 teaspoon coarsely crushed peppercorns	salt
	1 teaspoon cornstarch
1½ tablespoon *each* butter and oil	

Put steaks on a sheet of waxed paper and sprinkle on both sides with pepper. Cover with another sheet of paper and pound with a meat mallet, turning meat once, until pepper is embedded in the meat.

Heat butter and oil in a pan until very hot. Add the meat. Turn, salt, and cook until done to your favorite degree. (We prefer 2 minutes on each side for steaks about 1 inch thick—we like them rare.) Remove to warm serving dishes. Mix cornstarch and water, add to pan, and stir until sauce boils. Taste; add salt if necessary. Pour sauce over meat.

*STUFFED STEAK

2 boneless rib steaks cut ½ inch thick	¼ teaspoon salt
	dash of black pepper
¼ pound ground round steak	2 tablespoons butter
1 green onion, chopped	2 tablespoons red wine
1 tablespoon chopped parsley	1 teaspoon water
1 tablespoon brandy or cognac	

Have the butcher cut a slit in each steak to provide a pocket for stuffing. Mix the ground steak, onion, parsley, salt, and pepper well. Divide into two parts, stuff one portion in each steak, and skewer closed with a toothpick. Heat butter in a frying pan. Add the steaks and cook quickly, turning several times until both sides are browned. Remove to heated serving dishes. Add the wine, water, and brandy to the pan, and scrape the brownings. Pour over steaks, and serve. The ground round should be rare in the center.

*ENTRECÔTE WITH ROQUEFORT

2 boneless rib steaks, about ¾ pound each	1 tablespoon butter
2 tablespoons oil	2 tablespoons Roquefort cheese
	salt and pepper to taste

Rub steaks with oil, and pan-broil over very high heat 2 to 3 minutes on each side for rare; or cook longer according to your liking. (If you prefer, steaks can be cooked under the broiler.)

Cream the butter and Roquefort together until well blended. When steaks are done, put them on a serving platter or individual serving plates. Divide the butter-cheese mixture between the two, spreading it over the meaty portion (put more in the center of steaks, as it will melt and run off). Serve immediately.

BEEF CURRY

1 pound round steak, cut into 1-inch cubes	8-ounce can tomato sauce
¼ cup flour	1 cup water
2 tablespoons butter	1 tablespoon Worcestershire sauce
1 large onion, sliced	¼ teaspoon pepper
1½ teaspoons curry powder (or according to taste)	¼ teaspoon thyme
¼ teaspoon powdered ginger	1 teaspoon salt
1 clove garlic, mashed	9-ounce package frozen green beans

Coat meat cubes with flour. Heat butter in frying pan, add onion, curry, ginger, and garlic; cook until onion is tender. Push seasonings to one side of pan, and brown meat well on all sides. Add tomato sauce, water, Worcestershire, thyme, pepper, and salt; cover and simmer until meat is tender, about 1 hour. Add green beans and continue cooking until they are tender (about 10 minutes). Serve with hot rice. Also serve choice of condiments:

chopped nuts, raisins, coconut, chopped fresh tomatoes, cucumbers, chopped bananas, chopped apple, chutney, etc.

To serve four: Double the amount of meat, but use the same amount of seasonings, adding more to taste.

To serve six: Follow same procedure; double meat quantity but go easy with the seasonings, adding them to taste.

CHOPPED SALISBURY STEAK BURGUNDY

1 pound ground round steak	2 tablespoons butter or margarine
1 teaspoon salt	rine
⅛ teaspoon pepper	2 tablespoons salad oil
¼ cup flour	⅓ cup dry Burgundy

Mix meat, salt, and pepper. Blend well and shape into 2 large steaks. Sprinkle all sides with flour. Heat butter and oil in a frying pan over high heat. Add steaks and brown quickly on both sides; then lower heat and cook until as done as you like. Remove steaks from pan but keep them warm. Add Burgundy to pan and scrape bottom to loosen brownings. Bring to a boil and cook until thickened and reduced to about half. Pour this pan sauce over the steaks, and serve.

To serve four: Double all quantities.

To serve six: Triple all quantities except the fats; use 4 tablespoons each butter and oil.

Note: With salad and rolls, this makes a simple supper (see menu in front of book), or you can serve to 4 people as a late-evening snack after a movie, shaping the meat into 4 steaks instead of 2.

BEEF SHORT RIBS PIQUANT

½ medium-sized onion,
  chopped
1 tablespoon butter or margarine
½ cup water
¼ cup tomato catsup

1 tablespoon *each* vinegar,
  brown sugar, Worcestershire
  sauce, dry mustard
¼ teaspoon salt
1½ pounds beef short ribs, cut
  in 2½-inch pieces

flour, salt, pepper

Cook the onion in butter until golden brown. Add water, catsup, vinegar, brown sugar, Worcestershire sauce, mustard, and salt. Mix well; then simmer for 10 minutes.

Dredge meat with flour seasoned with salt and pepper. Brown on all sides in a frying pan with tight-fitting cover. Pour sauce over meat, cover, and bake in a slow oven (300°) for 2½ hours or until meat is tender. Serve with hot Fluffy Rice (see Index).

To serve four: Double all quantities.

To serve six: Triple the quantity of meat but double remaining quantities.

*MEAT AND EGGS IN INDIVIDUAL CASSEROLES

¾ cup ground cooked beef,
  pork, veal, chicken, or ham
2 tablespoons butter
1 small onion, finely chopped
2 teaspoons flour

⅓ cup beef broth or water
1½ teaspoons tomato catsup
salt and pepper to taste
2 eggs
paprika

chopped parsley and chives

This is an excellent suggestion for leftover meat.

Grind meat, measure, and have ready. Heat butter in pan and add onion; sauté for 2 minutes. Add meat, mix well, and sprinkle with the flour. Stir until blended. Add the broth and catsup and season with salt and pepper. Butter 2 individual casseroles and line with the beef mixture. Make an indentation in the center of each and crack an egg carefully into each center.

Bake in 350° oven for 5 to 10 minutes or until eggs are set to your liking. Sprinkle with paprika, parsley, and chives. Serve immediately.

*SPEEDY CHILI CON CARNE

1 tablespoon butter or margarine
¼ cup chopped onion
½ pound lean ground beef
1-pound can tomatoes

8-ounce can kidney beans, undrained
2 teaspoons (adjust according to taste) chili pepper
¼ teaspoon salt

dash of cayenne pepper

Melt butter and add onion and beef. Stir until it is browned. Add the tomatoes, beans, chili powder, salt, and pepper, and simmer 10 minutes. Serve hot.

*GROUND BEEFSTEAKS WITH CHEESE

½ pound lean ground beef
2 slices of a favorite cheese (Swiss, Cheddar, etc.)

1 tablespoon butter
salt and pepper to taste

Divide the meat into 4 patties. Lay a slice of cheese on each of two patties; cover with remaining patties, making two "sandwiches." Press together firmly. Melt butter in frying pan and cook patties 5 minutes on each side over medium-high heat. Season with salt and pepper.

CHILI (*for a cold winter evening*)

1 medium onion, chopped	1 tablespoon cornstarch
1 small clove garlic, crushed (optional)	2 tablespoons water
2 tablespoons salad oil	8-ounce can red kidney beans, undrained
¾ pound ground lean beef	2 cups hot cooked rice
½ teaspoon salt	1 avocado, sliced
1 teaspoon to 1 tablespoon chili powder, to taste	¼ head lettuce, shredded or thinly sliced
10½-ounce can beef broth	½ cup shredded sharp Cheddar cheese
2 tablespoons tomato catsup	

Sauté the onion and garlic in the oil until onion is tender. Add beef and cook until it is browned. Pour off excess fat; add salt, chili powder, beef broth, and catsup. Blend cornstarch and water and mix in; cook until thickened. Add the kidney beans. Simmer 10 minutes. Serve over hot cooked rice. Put the avocado, lettuce, and cheese on the table in a bowl, to sprinkle over the chili.

To serve four: Double all quantities.

To serve six: Triple all quantities except garlic and oil; use 2 cloves garlic and 4 tablespoons oil.

*STEAKS ON HORSEBACK

2 breakfast steaks (about 3 ounces each, boneless sirloin)	3 tablespoons butter
	4 eggs
salt and pepper	

Use two frying pans. Put half the butter in each. Heat one pan very hot and the other to medium heat. Quickly cook the steaks in the hot frying pan and arrange on individual serving dishes. Fry the eggs in the other pan—cover and cook them until the whites are set but yolks are still soft. Arrange 2 eggs on each steak. Pour butter remaining in the frying pan on top. Add salt and pepper to taste.

*HERB-MARINATED RIB EYE STEAK

½ cup red cooking wine	1 clove garlic, mashed
½ teaspoon *each* tarragon, basil, and rosemary	2 tablespoons salad or olive oil
	2 tablespoons lemon juice

2 rib eye steaks, 1 inch thick

Combine wine, tarragon, basil, rosemary, garlic, oil, and lemon juice. Pour over steaks and marinate 4 hours or more. Drain off marinade, and reserve. Broil or grill meat over hot coals until done to your liking, 5 to 7 minutes on each side for medium rare, 10 minutes on each side for medium. Baste with marinade while cooking. Add salt and pepper at the table.

*GROUND BEEFSTEAKS BORDELAISE

½ pound ground round steak	1 tablespoon flour
1 tablespoon butter or oil	½ cup red cooking wine, prefer-
1 small onion, finely chopped	ably a claret
(¼ cup)	salt and pepper

Shape the meat into 2 patties. Heat oil in pan. Add onion and cook over medium-high heat, stirring until golden (don't burn!). Add the meat; brown on both sides. Sprinkle with flour. Pour in the wine and stir sauce well. Lower heat and cook until sauce thickens. Add salt and pepper to taste. Put meat into serving dish and pour sauce over.

*GROUND BEEFSTEAKS WITH HAM

½ pound lean ground beef   1 tablespoon butter
2 teaspoons prepared mustard   1 teaspoon anchovy paste
2 slices boiled ham   salt and pepper

Shape meat into 4 thin patties. Spread with the mustard. Top two of the patties with ham. Press other two firmly over ham-topped patties, making 2 "sandwiches." Blend the butter and anchovy paste. Pan-broil the 2 "sandwiches" about 5 minutes on each side. Sprinkle with salt and pepper and top with the anchovy-butter mixture. Serve immediately.

*MACARONI BEEF CASSEROLE

½ pound ground beef,   1 tablespoon chopped parsley
   preferably round   dash of both pepper and
1 small onion, chopped   cinnamon
1 tablespoon butter   1 teaspoon salt (add more to
½ cup uncooked elbow-style   taste at table)
   macaroni   1 tablespoon flour
1 cup water   1 cup milk
¼ cup catsup   ½ teaspoon dry mustard
¼ cup shredded Cheddar cheese   1 egg, slightly beaten

In a large casserole combine the ground beef (crumble it up as you put it in), onion, butter, macaroni, water, catsup, cheese, parsley, pepper, cinnamon, and ½ teaspoon salt, mixing the ingredients together well with fork. In a saucepan combine the flour, milk, remaining salt, and mustard until well blended. Heat, stirring, until mixture is thickened. Beat in the egg quickly. Pour this mixture over the ground beef mixture. Mix lightly. Cover and bake in a moderate oven (350°) for 30 minutes. Remove cover and bake 5 minutes more. Let stand about 15 minutes before serving.

*SALTIMBOCCA

2 veal scallops or boneless veal   1 tablespoon oil
  chops, about ¾ pound   1 to 2 tablespoons butter
⅛ teaspoon crumbled sage
2 slices (about 4 inches square)
  prosciutto (Italian ham) or
  very thinly sliced smoked
  ham

Put veal between sheets of waxed paper and pound with a flat wooden mallet or flat side of meat mallet until meat is doubled in size in all directions. Sprinkle each flattened piece of meat with sage and top with ham. Pound again between paper until ham is "welded" into the meat. Roll each piece up tightly. Heat oil in pan and cook the rolls gently over moderate heat until meat is white. Add the butter and cook, turning the rolls once or twice, for 15 minutes. Serve immediately. Pour pan juices over the meat.

*MEXICALI MACARONI SKILLET

½ pound pork sausage   1 tablespoon sugar
⅓ cup diced onion   1½ teaspoons chili powder
⅓ cup diced green pepper   (more or less, according to
16-ounce can tomatoes   taste)
1 cup commercial sour cream   ½ teaspoon salt
          4 ounces elbow macaroni

In a frying pan, combine the sausage, onion, and green pepper, and brown. Drain off excess fat. Stir in the tomatoes, sour cream, sugar, chili powder, and salt. Add macaroni. Cover and simmer 20 to 30 minutes or until macaroni is tender.

*NIFTY-THRIFTY ONE-DISH MEAL

½ pound ground meat (lamb or beef)

1 small onion, chopped

1 small clove garlic, minced (optional)

1 tablespoon oil, if necessary

½ teaspoon salt

¼ teaspoon crumbled dried oregano

8-ounce can tomatoes (1 cup) or 2 fresh tomatoes, peeled and chopped

½ package (10-ounce size) frozen baby lima beans, partially thawed

1 medium-sized zucchini, sliced

hot rice

In a large frying pan, cook the meat with the onion and garlic until meat is brown and crumbly. Add the oil if the meat sticks to the pan. Season with the salt and oregano, and cook 5 minutes. Add the tomatoes, the baby lima beans, and zucchini. Cover and simmer 20 minutes. Serve over rice.

Note: Do not thaw entire package of limas. Cut package in half, wrap the unneeded portion well, and return it to the freezer.

*CHIPPED BEEF ON BAKED POTATO

2 medium-sized potatoes, scrubbed

butter or oil

½ cup dried chipped beef

1 cup medium White Sauce (see Index)

chives for garnish

Wipe potatoes dry and lightly rub with butter or oil. Bake in a moderate oven (375°) for 1 hour or until tender. Meanwhile, prepare the sauce. Soak the chipped beef in a small amount of water to remove some of the saltiness. Drain. Blend beef into the White Sauce. Cut potatoes open, fluff lightly with a fork, and spoon the meat sauce over. Garnish with a sprinkling of chopped chives.

*SAUSAGE-CORNMEAL CASSEROLE

6 tablespoons yellow cornmeal ½ cup shredded cheese
1½ cups milk   8 pork sausages or smoky
½ teaspoon salt   sausages, cooked brown
                    4 eggs

Combine the cornmeal, milk, and salt in a pan. Cook, stirring until thick. Spread in a shallow baking dish such as an 8-inch square pan, or divide between two individual-size casseroles. Sprinkle with grated cheese and arrange the browned sausages in a square formation on top. Break eggs into sausage squares, and bake at 375° for 30 minutes or until eggs are done to your taste.

GROUND BEEF AND CABBAGE

½ small head cabbage   ½ cup cooked rice
1 small onion, chopped   1 hard-cooked egg, chopped
2 tablespoons butter   ½ teaspoon salt
½ clove garlic, minced or   dash of pepper
   mashed   10-ounce can cream of tomato
¼ pound mushrooms, chopped   soup
¼ pound ground beef

Shred the cabbage. Brown the onion in butter; add the garlic, mushrooms, beef, rice, egg, salt, and pepper. Stir until well mixed. Blend the shredded cabbage in, then the cream of tomato soup. Turn into a shallow baking dish, about 1½-quart size. Bake in a moderate oven (350°) for 30 minutes. If needed, pour a little hot water over casserole to keep it from drying.

To serve four: Double all quantities and use a 2-quart casserole.

To serve six: Triple all quantities and use a 2½-quart casserole.

*GROUND BEEFSTEAK À L'ANCHOIS

½ pound ground round   1 teaspoon anchovy paste
1 teaspoon soft butter   1 tablespoon salad oil
                    salt and pepper

Shape meat into 4 thin patties. Spread 2 of them with the butter
and anchovy paste. Cover with the other two patties and press together. Add oil to pan. Cook patties 4 minutes on each side in hot
oil. Add salt (beware—anchovy paste is very salty!) and freshly
ground pepper. Serve immediately.

*FLAMBÉED VEAL CUTLETS WITH GRAPES

2 veal cutlets, ¼ pound each   salt and pepper
2 tablespoons butter   1 bunch (about 1 cup) seedless
⅓ cup dry white wine   grapes, cleaned of stems
                 2 tablespoons cognac or brandy

Put each cutlet between sheets of waxed paper. With the flat
side of a meat mallet, pound meat until it is doubled in length
and width, and very thin. Heat butter in a frying pan. Add cutlets
and brown well on both sides. Add the white wine, then sprinkle
with salt and pepper. Cover and cook over low heat for 10 minutes.

Add the grapes to the pan, and heat 2 minutes. Bring to the
table. Warm the cognac or brandy until just lukewarm. Pour it
over the meat, and ignite to flame.

*VEAL CUTLETS WITH ROQUEFORT

2 veal cutlets, about ¼ pound   1 egg, slightly beaten
    each   ½ cup dry bread crumbs
3 tablespoons soft butter   1 tablespoon oil
1 tablespoon Roquefort cheese   lemon wedges
flour   salt and pepper

Put cutlets between two sheets of waxed paper. Pound meat with the flat side of meat mallet until doubled in length and width. Cream the butter and Roquefort cheese. Spread mixture thinly over one side of each cutlet. Dip cutlets in flour, then in slightly beaten egg, then in bread crumbs. Fry quickly in hot oil for about 8 minutes, turning once. Serve with lemon wedges, adding salt and pepper to taste.

*BRAISED VEAL CHOPS

2 veal chops, about ½ pound each

2 tablespoons butter

1 tablespoon warmed cognac or brandy (optional)

2 carrots, peeled and sliced

salt and pepper to taste

Brown the chops in butter. Add cognac or brandy, and ignite. Add carrots. Sprinkle with salt and pepper. Reduce heat to low, cover, and cook for 30 minutes or until chops are tender. Put the chops on a platter and strain the sauce over them.

VEAL PAPRIKA

1 small onion, chopped

½ small clove garlic, mashed

1 tablespoon butter

¼ teaspoon salt

2 teaspoons paprika

1 small tomato, peeled and diced

¾ pound veal round, cut in cubes

1 cup commercial sour cream

hot noodles

Brown the onion and the garlic in butter. Add the salt, paprika, tomato, and veal. Cover and simmer for 45 minutes, stirring occasionally. When meat is tender, blend in the sour cream. Heat; don't boil. Serve over hot noodles.

To serve four: Double all quantities.

To serve six: Triple all quantities except sour cream; use 2 cups.

BREADED VEAL CUTLETS

2 boneless veal cutlets, about ¼   2 tablespoons flour
    pound each   ½ cup bread crumbs
1 egg, slightly beaten   ¼ cup butter
                     salt and pepper to taste

Put the cutlets between sheets of waxed paper and pound with
the flat side of a meat mallet until meat is very thin and twice the
original length and width. Break egg into a shallow dish. Dip
meat first in the flour, then in the beaten egg, then in bread crumbs.

Melt butter in a frying pan and add the cutlets. Cook on both
sides until golden, 8 to 10 minutes. Sprinkle with salt and pepper.

To serve four: Double all quantities but the egg.

To serve six: Triple all quantities but use 2 eggs.

SPICY VEAL SAUTÉ

1 pound veal shoulder, cubed   ¼ teaspoon thyme
1 tablespoon butter or   dash of Tabasco
    shortening   1 cup tomato catsup
1 clove garlic, mashed   2 tablespoons chopped stuffed
¼ teaspoon oregano   green olives
¼ teaspoon salt

In a heavy frying pan brown the veal cubes in butter until all
sides are golden. Add the garlic, oregano, salt, thyme, Tabasco,
catsup, and olives. Cover and simmer for 2 hours, or until veal is
very tender. Serve hot on Fluffy Rice.

To serve four: Double all quantities.

To serve six: Triple all quantities, but instead of using all tomato
catsup you can use tomato sauce for half of the 3 cups.

*GROUND VEAL BALLS IN SAUCE VERTE

1½ teaspoons butter
¼ cup finely chopped onion
½ medium head lettuce,
    chopped
¾ pound ground veal
¼ cup fine bread crumbs

½ cup milk
½ teaspoon salt
dash of nutmeg
butter for browning
Sauce Verte (see Index)

Melt the butter in a frying pan and add the onion and lettuce. Cook and stir over high heat until the lettuce is wilted. Put the mixture in a blender to purée, or press it through a fine sieve. Blend this purée with the veal, bread crumbs, milk, and nutmeg. Shape into balls about 1½ inches in diameter, and brown lightly in butter. Meanwhile, make the sauce. Place meatballs into two individual casseroles or a single 1-quart casserole. Pour sauce over them. Bake in a moderate oven (350°) for 20 minutes. Serve with boiled potatoes.

NORWEGIAN VEAL STEAK

2 veal steaks, about 4 ounces
    each
1 tablespoon shortening
salt and pepper to taste

½ cup commercial sour cream
¼ cup shredded gjetost
    (Norwegian brownish
    goat-milk cheese)

Pan-fry the steaks in the shortening on both sides, cooking until meat is golden and tender. Season with salt and pepper, and transfer to hot broiler-proof serving dishes. Blend the sour cream and cheese and heat slowly, stirring, until cheese is melted into the cream. Pour sauce over the veal steaks. Slip under broiler for 3 minutes or until top of sauce is lightly browned.

To serve four: Double all quantities.

To serve six: Triple all quantities, but instead of broiling steaks and sauce, add steaks to sauce and simmer for about 5 minutes; then serve hot.

WHITE WINE MARINATED LAMB ROAST

1 quart dry white wine	1 teaspoon salt
3 tablespoons black tea	1 teaspoon whole black pepper
3 teaspoons chopped fresh mint	2 to 4 pounds lamb roast (leg,
or dried mint leaves	rack, shoulder, or rib)
pinch of thyme	

Combine first six ingredients to make marinade. Pour it over meat and marinate for 3 days, turning meat occasionally. Drain off the marinade. Roast the meat until done to your liking, using a meat thermometer as a guide. Lamb should be roasted at 300° if done in the oven. If desired, it can be cooked over moderate coals on a spit.

RACK OF LAMB BOUQUETIÈRE

Rack of lamb is the specialty of many fine restaurants, and is often served for just two persons. Likewise, it is one of the best candidates for a "Cooking for Two" menu. The "rack" of lamb is comparable to the beef standing rib—it comes from the comparable part of the animal. You will use just half the rib section (the whole rib section is often used in a crown roast).

1 rack of lamb, 1½ to 2	1 small onion, sliced
pounds	½ teaspoon *each* thyme and
salt and pepper	crushed bay leaf
½ small clove garlic	1 cup white cooking wine
vegetables (see below)	

Have the butcher cut the rib bones to simplify carving. Sprinkle meat with salt and pepper. Cut the garlic into slivers and insert these under the fat layer on the outside of the rack. Put meat on a baking sheet (cover sheet with foil, and you save washing a pan later), with bones curving downward. Roast in a very hot oven (450°) for 25 minutes. Put onion, thyme, and bay leaf into the pan with the meat. Pour the wine over the meat. Roast 5 minutes more for medium-rare meat or 10 minutes more for meat that is medium-done. Transfer rack to a serving tray. Strain pan drippings and spoon them over the meat. Garnish with the vegetables.

Vegetables Bouquetière. Heat 2 tablespoons butter in a pan. Add ½ cup green peas, ¼ cup sliced carrot (1 small), and 1 cup cooked tiny new potatoes (or use canned ones). Cover and cook over medium heat, stirring occasionally, until carrots are done (about 10 minutes).

To serve four: Buy 2 racks of lamb and double all quantities; cooking time will be the same.

To serve six: Buy 3 racks of lamb and triple all quantities except the garlic (just double that). Cooking time will be the same.

*BARBECUED RACK OF LAMB

Here's another method for preparing rack of lamb, for barbecue enthusiasts.

1 rack of lamb, 1½ to 2 pounds   1 small clove garlic, sliced
                                                (optional)
              salt and freshly ground pepper

Have the butcher cut the bones on the rack from the backbone, to make carving easier. Cut slits in the fat layer and insert slices of garlic. Fold a piece of foil just large enough to protect bottom of the roast, and stand the rack of lamb on it on the barbecue grill. Cover barbecue and cook over very hot coals for 30 minutes. (If the barbecue is not the covered type, build a fire of medium-hot coals.) Cook rack for 15 minutes on each side, brushing with melted butter or oil to keep it moist. Sprinkle with salt and pepper before serving.

ROSEMARY RACK OF LAMB

Rosemary is a pungent herb that blends well with the flavor of lamb. Here you marinate the rack of lamb in a highly seasoned sauce, then barbecue or broil it until done. The longer you marinate it, the stronger the flavor.

1 cup *each* red cooking wine and cider vinegar	2 teaspoons crushed rosemary 1 rack of lamb, 1½ to 2 pounds
1 clove garlic, crushed	melted butter

Combine the wine, vinegar, garlic, and rosemary, and pour over the rack of lamb. Cover and marinate from 4 hours to overnight, depending on the desired strength of flavor. (First try the shorter marinade for mild flavor. You can save the marinade and try it again. Freeze marinade for storage.) Turn meat over once or twice while marinating. Barbecue over hot coals or broil about 8 inches from heat until done to your liking; brush with melted butter while cooking. Serve hot.

To serve four: Prepare two racks of lamb and cook in the same manner; double the marinade quantity.

To serve six: Buy three racks of lamb and prepare as above; However, you can probably get by with just double the amount of marinade.

*BROILED LAMB CHOPS

2 lamb rib chops, 1½ to 2 inches thick	salt and pepper butter
	mint, chopped

Sprinkle the lamb chops with salt and pepper on both sides, and spread with butter. Broil about 4 inches from source of heat until done to your liking—8 minutes on each side for well done. Sprinkle with chopped mint, fresh or dried, before serving.

*LAMB CHOPS, TARRAGON

¼ cup dry white table wine	2 shoulder lamb chops, 1 inch
1 teaspoon tarragon leaves	thick
dash of garlic salt	salt to taste

Combine the wine, tarragon, and garlic salt, and marinate the chops for an hour or longer in this mixture, turning once. Remove from marinade and broil or barbecue, 4 inches from the heat, basting once or twice with the remaining marinade. Allow 8 minutes on each side for well-done chops.

LAMB CHOPS WITH GJETOST SAUCE

2 large lamb chops, 1½ to 2 inches thick	¼ teaspoon oregano
1 tablespoon salad oil or olive oil	¼ cup shredded Norwegian gjetost
salt and freshly ground pepper	½ cup sour cream
	⅛ teaspoon salt

If you cannot buy large meaty lamb chops, choose 4 smaller ones and prepare 2 per serving. Rub each chop with oil; sprinkle with salt, freshly ground pepper, and oregano. Heat frying pan (lightly oiled) and add the chops. Cook over moderate heat until done to your liking.

Meanwhile, in a small pan combine the shredded gjetost (available in the cheese section of many supermarkets, this brownish goat's-milk cheese comes from Norway), sour cream, and salt, and heat slowly until the cheese is completely blended with the sour cream. Pour cheese sauce over cooked lamb chops to serve. Garnish with parsley if you wish.

To serve four: Double all quantities.

To serve six: Triple all quantities except oregano; add ½ teaspoon, and the next time you prepare the dish, add more if desired.

PLANKED LAMB CHOPS WITH VEGETABLES

1½ cups hot mashed potatoes   freshly ground pepper
  (dehydrated may be used)   1 cup buttered cooked peas
2 tablespoons soft butter   pinch of dried mint, crumbled
1 egg yolk   1 cup buttered cooked carrot
2 lamb chops, 1½ inches thick   slices
olive oil or salad oil   2 tablespoons butter

Blend the potatoes, soft butter, and egg yolk until smooth. Reserve. Arrange lamb chops on a baking sheet and rub with oil; sprinkle with pepper. Broil 6 inches from heat until done to your liking—about 5 minutes on each side for rare, 10 minutes for medium, and 12 minutes for well done. Arrange chops on a ½-inch hardwood plank (you can get one from a lumber company).

Surround the hot chops with the peas; then top peas with the mint. Arrange carrot slices decoratively around the peas. Dot with 2 tablespoons butter. Put mashed potatoes into a pastry bag and squeeze, or mound by spoonfuls, around the carrots to make a frame for the entire meal. Slip under broiler, about 10 inches from source of heat, and broil until top of potato is lightly browned. Serve hot.

To serve four: Double all quantities, and, using a larger plank, arrange meat and vegetables in manner similar to that described.

To serve six: Triple all quantities and arrange on large plank or a heatproof platter.

LAMB CHOPS WITH SOUR CREAM SAUCE

2 large lamb chops, 1 inch thick   ¼ teaspoon dry mustard
salt and pepper   1 tablespoon sherry
pinch dried tarragon   ¼ cup sour cream

Arrange lamb chops on broiler rack, and broil 5 minutes on each side for medium-rare chops, 8 to 10 minutes for well-done chops. Sprinkle with salt and freshly ground pepper. Keep hot. Combine tarragon, mustard, sherry, and sour cream, and heat through, stirring until blended. Pour sauce over the chops, and serve.

To serve four: Double all quantities.

To serve six: Triple all quantities except dry mustard; use ½ teaspoon.

BRAISED LAMB SHANKS

Lamb shanks are economical and yet rich in flavor. Serve them over Rice Pilaf, hot Fluffy Rice, or cooked wild rice.

2 lamb shanks	1 cup white cooking wine
flour	1 clove garlic, mashed
salt and pepper	pinch each of basil and oregano

Have the butcher crack the shank bones. Roll the shanks in flour and sprinkle with salt and pepper. Place them in a greased casserole and add the wine, garlic, basil, and oregano; cover. Bake in a moderate oven (350°) for 2 hours, or until meat is tender. Spoon pan drippings over the meat to serve.

To serve four: Double all quantities except garlic; use just 1 clove.

To serve six: Triple all quantities except garlic; use just 1 clove.

PORK TENDERLOIN IN PASTRY

1 whole pork tenderloin, about   prepared hot mustard
  ¾ pound   ¼ teaspoon tarragon, crushed
1 recipe single pastry crust (see
  Index or use pastry mix)

Trim off fat and wipe meat well. Roll pastry out to make a round about 12 inches in diameter. Spread with about 2 tablespoons mustard. Put meat on one end of the pastry, about 4 inches from the edge, and sprinkle with tarragon. Roll pastry around the meat, tucking the ends in to make the roll look like a fat sausage. Place on an ungreased baking sheet and bake in a moderate oven (350°) for 1 hour. Slice and serve hot, or chill, slice, and serve cold. This makes an excellent appetizer for a party.

To serve four: Choose a pork tenderloin weighing over 1 pound, and proceed as above with the same amount of ingredients.

To serve six: Choose a boneless 2-pound pork roast with a minimum of fat. Use recipe for double-crust pie. Bake for 1½ hours. Or make 2 rolls using 1- to 1½-pound pork tenderloin for each, and proceed as directed above.

 ## BROCHETTE OF PORK TENDERLOIN

1 pork tenderloin, about ¾   1 clove garlic, mashed
  pound   2 tablespoons sherry
¼ cup soy sauce   2 tablespoons cooking oil
1 tablespoon grated fresh ginger
  or ½ teaspoon powdered

Cut the tenderloin into pieces about 2 inches square, dividing it into 8 cubes. Put these in a bowl. Combine soy sauce, ginger, garlic, sherry, and oil, and pour the mixture over the meat. Toss well, cover, and marinate for 2 to 3 hours, or longer for stronger flavor. String meat cubes on two skewers (the Oriental-style bamboo skewers are handy, if you can get them), leaving space between the pieces. Place skewers over a pan on a rack, and bake in a very hot oven (450°) for 20 minutes or until meat is browned and glazed.

To serve four: Double the amount of meat, but keep amounts of marinade ingredients the same.

To serve six: Triple the amount of meat, but double the amounts of marinade ingredients.

PORK TENDERLOIN AND MUSHROOMS

4 tablespoons soy sauce
1 small clove garlic, mashed
1 teaspoon grated fresh ginger
  or ¼ teaspoon powdered
1 tablespoon brown sugar

1 tablespoon salad oil
¾ pound pork tenderloin, cut in
  1-inch strips
¾ pound fresh mushrooms,
  sliced

Combine the soy sauce, garlic, ginger, and brown sugar. (Do this any time in advance.) Heat the oil in a frying pan until very hot, and add the pork tenderloin. Stir and fry the meat until lightly browned on all sides (3 to 5 minutes). Add the soy mixture and stir until blended. Cover and cook over medium heat for 15 minutes. Add the mushrooms, turn heat to high, and stir and cook until mushrooms are tender, about 5 minutes. Liquid should be almost gone from the pan. Serve over rice.

For four servings: Double all quantities except garlic; use just 1 clove.

For six servings: Triple all quantities except garlic; use just 1 clove.

*MUSTARD-GLAZED SMOKED PORK CHOPS

1 tablespoon cooking oil or
   salad oil
2 smoked pork chops

2 teaspoons prepared mustard
2 tablespoons peach or apricot
   jam

Heat oil in a heavy frying pan. Brown pork chops on both sides. Cover and cook for 10 minutes. Smoked pork chops are usually fully cooked and need only to be heated through. Transfer the chops from pan to serving plates. Stir the mustard and jam into the pan juice, blending well. Pour this over the meat as a glaze.

*GLAZED PORK CHOPS

2 large pork chops, 1 inch thick
2 tablespoons tomato catsup

2 tablespoons orange juice
dash of salt

Brown the pork chops on both sides in a heavy frying pan with cover. Drain off excess fat. Combine catsup, orange juice, and salt, and pour over the chops. Cover and simmer slowly for 45 minutes. Spoon drippings over pork chops to serve.

*PORK CHOPS WITH ORANGE

2 pork chops, 1 inch thick
2 teaspoons soy sauce
pinch of dry mustard
1/4 teaspoon ground ginger
1/4 teaspoon salt

1 teaspoon sugar, white or
   brown
1 large orange or 2 small
   oranges
3 tablespoons granulated sugar

Trim fat from the pork chops and melt it in a frying pan. In a small bowl, combine the soy sauce, mustard, ginger, salt, and 1 teaspoon sugar. Rub the mixture into the chops. Brown chops well in the pan coated with the rendered fat. Reduce heat to low, cover, and cook chops for 45 minutes. Remove to serving plates and keep them hot. Meanwhile, cut the peel from the orange. Cut orange into thick slices, sprinkle with the 3 tablespoons sugar, and brown slices quickly in the frying pan, adding butter if more fat is needed. Arrange orange slices on pork chops, and serve.

*HAM STEAK TARRAGON

Tarragon Sauce (see Index)
2 tablespoons butter

4 slices cooked ham, ¼ inch
   thick, 3 inches square

Make the sauce and keep it hot. Melt the butter in a frying pan. Add the ham slices and heat (don't fry). Arrange on warm serving dishes, pour the sauce over the meat, and serve hot.

*HAM BEEF ROLLS

¼ pound ground round
2 tablespoons milk
2 tablespoons dry bread crumbs
2 tablespoons chopped onion
dash *each* of salt and pepper
1 large thin slice ham steak,
   about ¼ inch thick (bone
   removed)

2 whole cloves
1 tablespoon butter
¼ cup brown sugar
1 tablespoon cornstarch
1 teaspoon prepared mustard
¼ cup orange juice
1 cup crushed pineapple

Mix the ground round, milk, crumbs, onion, salt, and pepper. Spread the mixture over the ham steak, and roll ham up. Press whole cloves into ham roll. Skewer with toothpicks to hold shut. Melt the butter in a pan; add the sugar, cornstarch, mustard, orange juice, and pineapple. Place the ham roll in a long, narrow baking dish, and pour the fruit mixture on top. Bake in a moderate oven (350°) for 30 minutes. Baste well and bake for 15 minutes more. Cut roll in half to serve.

HAM SOUFFLÉ

2 tablespoons butter	dash of pepper
2 tablespoons flour	3 egg yolks
1 cup milk	1 cup finely chopped or ground
⅛ teaspoon salt	ham

3 egg whites, beaten stiff

Heat butter in a pan. Add flour and mix well. Blend in the milk, salt and pepper, and cook, stirring until thickened and smooth. Cool to lukewarm. Add egg yolks, one at a time, beating after each addition. Stir in the ham. Fold in the beaten egg whites, and then pour the mixture into a buttered 2- or 3-cup soufflé dish or straight-sided casserole, or 2 individual soufflé dishes 1 to 1½ cups in size. Bake in a moderately hot oven (375°) for 20 to 25 minutes.

To serve four: Double all quantities and use a 1-quart baking dish. Bake for 30 minutes.

To serve six: Triple all quantities and use a 2-quart soufflé dish for baking; bake for 35 to 40 minutes.

*BROCHETTE OF SAUSAGES

10 small precooked link sausages	8 small cherry tomatoes or 2 large ones, quartered
8 mushroom caps	
1 tablespoon cooking or salad oil	

Alternate sausages, mushroom caps brushed with oil, and tomatoes on skewers. Cook over barbecue grill or 6 inches beneath broiler until meat is heated through and mushroom caps are lightly browned, turning skewers occasionally. Serve with hot mustard.

*SAUSAGE-CHEESE-PINEAPPLE KEBABS

Fun for a picnic! Take along a throw-away foil pan to use as a barbecue pot; also a cake rack and about 8 charcoal briquets. If you put the briquets in a tight-lidded can and soak them with lighter fluid, they will be ready to start quickly. At home, assemble the kebabs and cook them at your picnic site. Also a great idea for a breakfast picnic on a beautiful summer morning.

6 smoky link sausages,   6 chunks fresh pineapple (or
  precooked   canned, if you must)
6 cubes sharp Cheddar cheese

Assemble the ingredients on two skewers (the imported Oriental bamboo skewers are excellent), alternating the items. Cook over hot coals until sausages are browned and cheese has melted slightly.

*HAM-CHEESE-PINEAPPLE KEBABS

Prepare the kebabs as in preceding recipe, but instead of smoky sausage links, skewer 1½-inch cubes of cooked ham along with the cheese and pineapple. Cook over coals as directed, or cook under broiler until heated through.

*SAUSAGE SOUBISE

1 pound pork sausage   1 cup white cooking wine,
1 large onion, chopped   preferably sauterne
1 tablespoon flour   salt and pepper to taste
        hot Wheat Pilaf (see Index)

Crumble the pork sausage into a frying pan and cook over moderate heat, stirring until cooked through. Drain off all fat. Add onion to the pan and cook until it is tender. Add the flour and wine, and blend thoroughly. Cook until mixture is thickened. Taste and add seasoning accordingly. Serve over hot Wheat Pilaf.

MARINADE AU VIN FOR GAME AND VENISON

If there is a hunter in the family, try this marinade, which is intended to enhance rather than cover up the flavor of venison, bear, moose, and elk.

4 tablespoons oil	4 sprigs parsley
1 onion, chopped	1 quart white or red wine
2 medium-sized carrots, peeled and chopped	1 cup wine vinegar
	pinch of thyme
1 clove garlic, minced	1 bay leaf
1 stalk celery, chopped	1 teaspoon salt

1 teaspoon whole pepper

Heat the oil in a large pan. Add the vegetables and stir until they are browned. Add remaining ingredients and bring to a boil. Reduce heat and simmer 45 minutes. While this marinade is boiling hot, pour it over the meat. Marinate meat several hours or overnight, according to the cut it is, before roasting or grilling it until done. This marinade can be used on all cuts of game, the tenderest and the toughest. Makes 1 quart.

*VENISON SCALLOPINE

2 thin slices venison round steaks, about 3 inches square, 1/4 inch thick	flour
	1/4 cup butter
	1/2 cup dry red cooking wine
salt and pepper	salt and pepper to taste

Put the venison slices between two sheets of waxed paper, and pound with the flat side of a meat mallet (or a wooden mallet or solid rolling pin) until meat is about doubled in length and width. (Long pounding produces tenderer meat.) Sprinkle the meat with salt; pepper lightly and then dust with flour on both sides. Melt the butter in a heavy skillet. Cook the meat quickly on both sides until lightly browned. Add the wine, cover, and simmer for 15 minutes. Add salt and pepper to taste, and serve.

LIVER AND BACON PATTIES

Surprise! Even liver can be considered a fine meat to serve by candlelight. But you'll be more likely to serve these patties as rather everyday fare. Liver is very tasty prepared according to this recipe, and the problem of tough membranes is eliminated.

1 slice bacon, cooked and
  crumbled (reserve
  drippings)
½ pound liver, ground
1 tablespoon minced onion

¼ teaspoon salt
dash of pepper
2 tablespoons flour
1 egg, beaten
bacon drippings or butter

Combine the bacon, ground liver (ask butcher to grind it), onion, salt, pepper, flour, and egg. Drop spoonfuls of the mixture into frying pan with bacon drippings. (The mixture is of batter-like consistency.) Cook, turning once, until meat is well browned on both sides. Serve with sweet pickle slices.

To serve four: Double all quantities except egg; use just 1.

To serve six: Triple all quantities except egg; use 2 eggs.

Poultry

Many of the finest dishes are adaptable to our very plentiful—and often low-priced—chicken. Here are some of my favorites; you'll recognize that many of them sound similar to certain veal recipes. In fact, many veal recipes are excellent when made with chicken breasts.

Recipes for duck, pheasant, and Cornish game hen are included here too because it is often hard to find directions for cooking these birds. We have an acquaintance who raises pheasants, and when I began looking for recipes, I found they were almost as scarce as the bird.

Recipes that can be doubled or tripled without further instruction are marked with an asterisk (*).

*ASSEMBLE-AHEAD CHICKEN BAKE

A marvelous dish to serve when time is short before dinner. Assemble the whole thing ahead—either in the morning or the night before—so that you can slip it into the oven practically as soon as you get home. Just allow time for the oven to heat. For company, double or triple the amounts.

½ frying chicken, cut up, *or* 2 to 4 breast pieces, *or* 2 each of chicken thighs and legs
1 egg, beaten

1 cup flour mixed with 1 teaspoon salt
butter
½ cup milk or light cream
paprika

Wash chicken pieces and pat them dry. Dip in egg and then in the seasoned flour, and lay side by side in a casserole. Add a piece of butter to the dish—about a tablespoon—if desired. Cover with waxed paper, and refrigerate until cooking time.

Remove casserole from refrigerator. Heat oven to 400°. Put casserole of chicken into oven, uncovered, and bake for 10 minutes. Pour on the milk or cream and sprinkle lightly with paprika. Return to oven, lower heat to 350°, and bake for 30 minutes more or until chicken is tender when pierced with a fork and juices run clear. If necessary, add more milk or cream.

COQ AU VIN

½ frying chicken, cut up	¼ cup chopped green onion
salt and pepper	1 small clove garlic, mashed
2 slices bacon, cut in ½-inch pieces	1 tablespoon flour
	1 cup dry red wine
1 tablespoon butter	1 tablespoon coarsely chopped
2 small onions, chopped	parsley
¼ pound mushrooms, sliced	pinch of thyme
parsley for garnish	

Sprinkle chicken pieces with salt and pepper. Cook the bacon until crisp. Remove bacon. Add butter to bacon fat, and brown the chicken slowly in fat until golden on all sides. Add the onions and mushrooms, and cook until tender. Add green onion and garlic. Pour off all but 1 to 2 tablespoons of fat. Blend in the flour, then add wine. Cook, stirring occasionally, until sauce boils. Add parsley and thyme. Cover and simmer 30 minutes or until chicken is tender but not overcooked. Serve garnished with parsley.

To serve four: Double all the quantities.

To serve six: Triple all the quantities except garlic. Actually, it is wise just to double all seasonings at first, and taste. Then add more if you think it is necessary.

*MOCK BARBECUED CHICKEN

This chicken simmers in a barbecue sauce in a skillet or frying pan right on top of the stove, or in an electric frypan.

½ frying chicken, cut up (½ breast, ½ back, 1 thigh, 1 leg)	2 tablespoons catsup
	½ teaspoon Worcestershire sauce
2 tablespoons salad oil	⅛ teaspoon garlic salt
1 tablespoon vinegar	½ teaspoon salt
1 tablespoon brown sugar	¼ teaspoon pepper

¼ cup water

Wash chicken pieces and pat them dry. In a frying pan combine the oil, vinegar, sugar, catsup, Worcestershire, garlic salt, salt, pepper, and water. Add chicken pieces and cook uncovered over medium heat, turning to brown evenly. Cook for 35 to 40 minutes or until tender. Remove to a warm platter. Skim the oil from the sauce in the pan. Add a bit of water and stir to loosen brownings. Pour sauce over chicken and serve at once.

BROILED DEVILED CHICKEN

1 broiler-fryer, cut lengthwise (small size, less than 2 pounds)	2 tablespoons olive oil
	½ small onion, minced
	2 tablespoons minced parsley
1 teaspoon salt	1 tablespoon olive oil
dash of cayenne pepper	¼ cup dry white cooking wine

Wash and dry the chicken. Combine salt, cayenne, and 2 tablespoons olive oil, and rub onto chicken on all sides. Broil about 6 inches from the heat, cut side up, for 15 minutes. (Check carefully to see that points that stick up do not begin to burn. If necessary, lower the broiler rack.) Turn chicken over and spread with a mixture of the minced onion, parsley, and 1 tablespoon olive oil. Broil another 15 minutes or until juices run clear when chicken is pierced with a fork. Transfer to a hot platter. Add the dry white wine to the broiling pan and stir to loosen all the brownings. Pour juices over the chicken. Serve with an herb-buttered pasta, Wheat Pilaf, rice, or wild rice (see chapter "Rice, Wild Rice, Bulgur Wheat, and Pasta").

To serve four: Double all the quantities, or use a heavier chicken and serve the chicken quartered.

To serve six: Triple all quantities; again, if you wish, serve the chicken quartered. Some broiler-fryers weigh about 3 pounds, and they make healthy servings when quartered.

*BAKED CHICKEN CASSEROLE

½ chicken, cut up, *or* 2 chicken breasts, split, *or* 2 legs and 2 thighs
salt, pepper, paprika
1 tablespoon butter
2 tablespoons *each* flour and water

½ cup dry white wine
1 cup sliced fresh mushrooms
¼ cup sliced stuffed green olives
2 tablespoons minced parsley
¼ cup chopped salted mixed nuts

Wash chicken pieces and pat them dry. Sprinkle with salt, pepper, and paprika. Heat butter in heavy pan, add chicken, and sauté until golden on all sides. Transfer the chicken to a casserole dish. Add the flour to pan drippings, mixing well. Add the water, wine, and mushrooms. Cook and stir until mushrooms are tender (3 minutes). Add the olives and parsley, and pour sauce over the chicken. Sprinkle nuts on top, cover, and bake in a moderately hot oven (375°) for 30 minutes. Remove cover and bake an additional 5 minutes.

SHOYU CHICKEN

This tasty variation on chicken has an Oriental flavor. Serve it, if you wish, with fried rice, which comes frozen or canned for convenience.

½ chicken, cut up, *or* 2 large   3 tablespoons brown sugar
  breast pieces *or* 4 small ones,   ¼ cup vinegar
  or 2 legs and 2 thighs   1 tablespoon *each* cornstarch
1 tablespoon salad oil   and water
3 tablespoons soy sauce

Wash chicken and pat it dry. Brown over medium heat in the oil until golden on all sides. Combine the soy sauce, brown sugar, and vinegar and pour over the chicken. Cover and simmer for 30 minutes or until chicken is tender. Remove chicken to serving plate and keep warm. Combine the cornstarch and water, and stir it into the liquid in the pan. Stir and cook until thickened. Pour over chicken and serve.

To serve four: Use one whole chicken (cut up) and just 1 tablespoon oil for browning, but double the remaining ingredients.

To serve six: Use one large frying chicken (cut up), or a "three-legged" or "three-breasted" chicken (some butchers pack this way especially for customers who need the equivalent of 1½ chickens). Use 2 tablespoons oil for browning the chicken, and triple the remaining ingredients. Cooking time will be about the same, once the chicken is browned.

*FLAMBÉED CHICKEN

1 small broiler-fryer (1½ to 1¾   salt and pepper
  pounds), halved   2 tablespoons brandy or cognac
4 tablespoons butter   ¼ cup heavy cream
            1 egg yolk

Brown chicken in the butter. Sprinkle with salt and pepper. Cover and cook over medium-low heat for 30 minutes. Chicken should be cooked by this time. Check by pricking with a fork or pointed knife. If fluid flows out clear, the chicken is done.

Pour the brandy over it and touch with a lighted match. Mix cream and egg yolk, pour over chicken, and stir to loosen brownings from pan. (Don't let sauce boil.) Transfer chicken to serving dish. Stir sauce until smooth. Taste, then add salt and pepper. Pour sauce over chicken, and serve.

*CHICKEN CORDON BLEU

4 pieces chicken breast meat, about ½ to ¾ pound total	flour
	¼ cup butter
1 slice Swiss cheese	½ cup dry white table wine
2 slices thinly sliced ham	pinch each of sage and basil
salt and pepper	¼ cup heavy cream

Put a piece of the boned chicken breast meat between two sheets of waxed paper. Pound with the flat side of a meat mallet or with a wooden mallet until meat is doubled in length and width and is very thin. Repeat for all four pieces.

Cut the cheese slice in half. Lay each half on a piece of the chicken meat. Cover each with a slice of ham. Top ham and cheese with remaining pieces of chicken, and press together to make two firm "packages." Pound lightly so that they stay together.

Sprinkle "packages" lightly with salt and pepper, and roll them in flour. Heat butter in pan. Brown meat on both sides until golden, over high heat. Cook for 3 to 4 minutes on each side, remove from pan to warm serving plates, and keep warm. Add wine to pan and boil down to about half. Add the sage, basil, and cream. Stir until smooth and the brownings from the pan are dissolved in the sauce. Pour over meat, and serve.

*CHICKEN CUTLETS RUSSE

¾ to 1 pound chicken breasts,   ½ teaspoon salt
  boned   1 tablespoon soft butter
1 slice white bread   dash *each* of pepper and nutmeg
⅓ cup light cream   1 egg, slightly beaten
               fine dry bread crumbs

Have butcher remove the bones from the chicken breasts. (Some stores regularly carry boned chicken breasts.) Put the meat through a food chopper, using the finest blade. Soak the bread in the cream; then combine with the ground chicken. Add the salt, butter, pepper, and nutmeg, and mix until well blended. Shape into 4 patties. Roll these in beaten egg, then in the bread crumbs, and cook in butter in frying pan over medium to high heat for 5 minutes on each side. Serve with Mushroom Sauce (see Index).

BROILED SKEWERED CHICKEN BREASTS

1 whole chicken breast, halved   ¼ teaspoon dry mustard
¼ cup *each* soy sauce, sherry,   ½ clove garlic, mashed
  and pineapple juice   2 onions, quartered
1 teaspoon ground ginger   12 chunks pineapple
        1 small green pepper, quartered

Remove bones from the chicken breast and put meat in a bowl. Combine the soy sauce, sherry, and pineapple juice with ginger, mustard, and garlic. Pour over the chicken. Marinate for 1 hour or more, as desired. Meanwhile, prepare the onion, pineapple, and green pepper by boiling the onion and green pepper for 1 minute, then cooling.

Drain chicken breasts, cut each into three pieces, and alternate pieces on two skewers with onion, pineapple, and green pepper.

Cook over hot coals or 6 inches from broiler until meat and vegetables are golden on all sides. Brush occasionally with the marinade. Cooking time will be about 15 to 20 minutes.

To serve four: Double all quantities.

To serve six: Triple all ingredients but garlic; double the garlic.

CHICKEN-FILLED CRÊPES

4 large thin pancakes, 6 or 7 inches in diameter
½ cup thick White Sauce (see Index)
1 tablespoon sherry, or 1 teaspoon lemon juice
1 cup finely diced cooked chicken
¼ cup finely chopped blanched almonds
1 tablespoon finely minced green onion
⅓ cup mayonnaise
1 egg white stiffly beaten
2 tablespoons grated Parmesan or Romano cheese

Prepare the pancakes (for this you can use your own favorite recipe), Combine the White Sauce, sherry, chicken, almonds, and onion. Divide the mixture between the pancakes, spreading it on each one. Roll up like jelly rolls. Place two rolls in each individual serving dish or on ovenproof dinner plates. Fold mayonnaise into the egg white. Spread this mixture over the pancake rolls. Sprinkle with the cheese. Bake in a moderately hot oven (375°) for 10 minutes.

To serve four: Double all quantities; pancakes can be baked in a shallow casserole.

To serve six: Triple all quantities, and again, use a large shallow casserole if you wish. Baking time in any case will be the same.

CHICKEN WINGS WITH RICE

You can cook this in an electric skillet if you have one; otherwise a heavy frying pan will do.

6 chicken wings, disjointed	1 stalk celery, diced
¼ cup flour	½ cup chopped green onions
½ teaspoon salt	½ cup uncooked rice
dash of black pepper	1¼ cups chicken broth
3 tablespoons butter	⅛ teaspoon thyme

½ cup toasted almonds

Wash and dry chicken wings; use heavy knife to disjoint them at the elbow. Discard tips. Combine flour, salt, and pepper in a paper bag. Add chicken wings and shake to coat well. Melt butter in heavy pan. Brown wings slowly until they are golden on all sides. Remove, and add the celery, onion, and rice to the pan. Sauté rice until it is toasted and golden. Add the chicken broth and thyme. Stir well. Return wings to pan. Cover and simmer slowly for 20 to 25 minutes. Serve topped with slivered toasted almonds.

To serve four: Cook 1 small (about 2-pound) chicken, cut up as directed, but double all other ingredients.

To serve six: Buy a "triple-breasted" or "triple-legged" chicken (some butchers put them up this way), or 2 small cut-up chickens. (You have to use your own judgment of how hungry your eaters will be!) Triple the other ingredients. Cooking time will remain about the same.

CHICKEN BREASTS MILANESE

This dish is very similar to Chicken Scallopine. The distinction is in the use of lemon and parsley for flavoring. The "flattening" process makes the breast meat extremely tender, and the flavor and texture are delicate and delightful.

¾ pound boned chicken breast meat

salt and pepper

flour

¼ cup butter

¼ cup chicken broth (canned or homemade)

½ cup heavy cream

juice of 1 lemon

chopped fresh parsley

Put boned chicken breast pieces between two sheets of waxed paper. Pound with flat side of meat mallet or wooden mallet until meat is doubled in length and width, and very thin. Sprinkle with salt, pepper, and flour. Heat butter in frying pan and brown meat quickly on both sides. Add chicken broth and simmer 5 minutes. Remove meat to a serving platter or plates. Boil liquid until reduced by half; add cream and bring to a boil again, cooking until sauce is thickened. Sprinkle meat with juice from lemon and pour sauce over. Sprinkle liberally with chopped fresh parsley. Serve immediately.

*FRIED CHICKEN

How to fry chicken is a subject of controversy. This is my favorite method.

½ chicken, cut up (about 1½ pounds)

milk

½ cup flour

½ teaspoon *each* salt and pepper

1 beaten egg

cracker crumbs

hot fat, about 2 inches deep

Wash chicken and pat it dry. Dip pieces in milk, then in the flour mixed with salt and pepper, then in the beaten egg, then in cracker crumbs. Cook them in hot fat (about 375°) until golden on both sides (no longer than 10 minutes). Remove smaller pieces and breast pieces after 5 minutes and check for doneness. It's a shame to get the breast meat so dry and overcooked that it has no flavor. Serve hot or cold. This is excellent picnic fare.

CHICKEN BREASTS IN CREAM

1 large chicken breast, halved	¼ cup heavy cream
1 tablespoon *each* oil and butter	1 egg yolk
2 green onions, finely chopped	lemon juice, salt, and pepper to
2 tablespoons cognac or brandy	taste

Remove skin and bones from the chicken breasts. Heat oil and butter in small frying pan over moderate heat. Add chicken, and cook, turning occasionally, for 5 minutes. Then add onion, and cook another 3 to 5 minutes. Transfer to heated serving dishes and keep hot. Add the cognac to juices in pan. Bring to a boil and stir to loosen the brownings from the pan. Blend the cream and egg yolk, add to the pan, and simmer and stir for 3 minutes. Taste, then add lemon juice, salt, and pepper. Pour over chicken breasts, garnish with parsley, and serve.

To serve four: Double all quantities.

To serve six: Triple all ingredients except oil and butter; just double those.

*CHICKEN POJARSKI

¾ pound boned chicken breasts	nutmeg
(about 3 halves)	1 teaspoon salt
1 cup soft bread crumbs	flour
⅓ cup milk	1 egg, beaten
½ cup soft butter	fine dry bread crumbs
⅓ cup heavy cream	⅓ cup butter
	fresh lemon

Remove skin from chicken and chop meat fine or put through food chopper, using a fine blade. Put bread crumbs in a bowl. Add the milk and blend in the chopped chicken. Add the butter and cream, mixing well. Add salt and a dash of nutmeg. Divide into 6 portions. Shape each into a patty and roll in flour, then in beaten egg, then in fine bread crumbs. Cook patties in butter over moderate heat until golden on both sides (20 minutes). Pour pan juice over the patties. Squeeze lemon over each, and serve.

*WILD RICE AND CHICKEN LIVERS

This makes a great main dish for a little meal. Use individual casseroles or *au gratin* dishes to serve it good and hot—if you have them. Otherwise, bake it in a 1-quart casserole—or a pie pan will do nicely.

1 cup cooked wild rice (see Index for cooking directions)	2 tablespoons butter
pinch of thyme	½ pound chicken livers, chopped
dash of pepper	salt to taste
1 green onion, finely chopped	2 tablespoons melted butter
2 tablespoons dry bread crumbs	

Cook the wild rice, adding the thyme and pepper, and have ready. In the meantime, cook the green onion in the butter in a heavy frying pan. Add the chicken livers and cook, stirring lightly, until livers are cooked through but not overcooked so that they become dry. Fold the cooked rice into the chicken livers; taste, add salt if needed, and turn into two individual casseroles about 1½ cups in size, or into a 3- or 4-cup casserole. Blend the melted butter and bread crumbs and sprinkle over. Bake in a moderate oven (350°) for 15 minutes or until heated through.

Note: You can prepare this casserole ahead except for the baking; keep it covered in the refrigerator until you wish to heat it. Heating time will be approximately 30 minutes from refrigerator temperature.

*CHICKEN SCALLOPINE

¾ pound boned chicken breast   ¼ cup butter
  meat   ½ cup each dry white table
salt and pepper   wine and heavy cream
flour   ¼ teaspoon basil leaves
          1 cup sliced fresh mushrooms

Put boned chicken breast pieces between two sheets of waxed paper. Pound with flat side of a meat mallet or with a wooden mallet until meat is doubled in length and width, and is very thin. Sprinkle with salt, pepper, and flour. Heat butter in frying pan and brown meat quickly on both sides. Add the wine and simmer 15 minutes. Remove meat from pan to serving plates and keep it hot. Boil liquid down until reduced by half. Add the cream and basil, and bring to a boil again. Add the mushrooms and cook for 5 minutes, stirring. Spoon sauce over meat.

INDIVIDUAL CHICKEN POT PIES

1 tablespoon butter   1 egg yolk
4 medium-sized fresh   ¼ cup light cream
  mushrooms   1½ cups diced cooked chicken
4 bulb ends of green onions,   or turkey
  chopped   salt and pepper to taste
½ package frozen green peas   pastry for 1 crust pie (your own,
1 cup chicken broth   or use a mix)
1 teaspoon Worcestershire   milk for brushing pastry

Leftover baked, boiled, or barbecued chicken or turkey can be used for this dish.

Heat butter in frying pan. Add mushrooms, onion, and peas. Cook, stirring, over medium-high heat until vegetables are hot. Add broth and Worcestershire. Blend egg yolk and cream and add to mixture, along with the chicken. Heat through. Taste; then add salt and pepper. Divide between 2 individual-size baking dishes, or put into an 8-inch pie pan. Roll out crust, fit it over filling, and seal to edge of dish. Brush top with milk and bake in a hot oven (425°) for 20 minutes or until crust is golden.

To serve four: Double all quantities and divide between 4 individual casseroles, about 8-ounce size. Or put into a 1-quart casserole.

To serve six: Triple all quantities and divide between 6 individual dishes, or put into a 1½-quart casserole.

BAKED CHICKEN SALAD

1 cup diced cooked chicken
1 cup diced celery
½ cup mayonnaise
¼ cup chopped walnuts

1 tablespoon lemon juice
1 tablespoon minced onion
salt and pepper to taste
bread crumbs

Combine the chicken, celery, mayonnaise, nuts, lemon juice, and onion. Taste; then add salt and pepper. Turn into a shallow casserole or two individual casseroles. Sprinkle with bread crumbs and bake in a very hot oven (450°) for 15 minutes or until dish is lightly browned.

To serve four: Double all quantities and bake in a 1½-quart casserole.

To serve six: Triple all quantities and bake in a 2-quart casserole, adding 5 minutes to baking time.

*GLAZED CHICKEN BREASTS SUISSE

1 tablespoon butter	2 tablespoons dry white wine or
1 whole chicken breast,	water
halved	2 teaspoons lemon juice
½ teaspoon salt	¼ cup shredded Swiss cheese
dash of pepper	2 tablespoons slivered blanched
4 tablespoons currant jelly	almonds

Heat butter in a heavy frying pan that has a cover. Add the chicken breasts and sauté until golden on both sides. Sprinkle with the salt and pepper. Combine the jelly, wine or water, and lemon juice, and beat until blended. Pour mixture over the chicken, cover, lower heat, and simmer until chicken is tender—about 25 minutes. If overcooked, the chicken will be dry. Remove from heat. Sprinkle with cheese and almonds, then slip under broiler about 6 inches from source of heat, and broil until the cheese is melted and top is golden brown.

If desired, put the chicken breasts into individual *au gratin* dishes before broiling, pour sauce over, sprinkle with cheese and almonds, and broil until golden.

CHICKEN LIVERS AVOCADO

Serve this flavorful mixture on toast or in baked patty shells.

2 tablespoons butter or	½ pound fresh or frozen
margarine	chicken livers
1 small onion, chopped	1 ripe avocado, diced
½ small green pepper, chopped	¾ cup commercial sour cream
1 small clove garlic, mashed	salt and pepper to taste

In frying pan, melt the butter and add onion, green pepper, and garlic; stir over moderate heat for about half a minute. Add the chicken livers (if frozen, thaw first) and cook, stirring occasionally, for 10 minutes or until livers are just done (not overcooked). Add avocado and stir in sour cream. Blend carefully and continue cooking until heated through. Taste, and add salt and pepper. Serve immediately. This makes an excellent quick meal.

To serve four: Double all quantities but the garlic, which can be optional anyway.

To serve six: Again, do not add more garlic, but triple the remaining quantities. Be careful not to agitate the mixture too much after the avocado is added or it will become mushy. When tripling this recipe, you can get by with just two avocados, although if you're fond of them you won't want to.

*CHICKEN BREASTS IN WINE SAUCE

1 whole chicken breast, split   ½ cup sour cream
1 cup Béchamel Sauce (see   ¼ cup dry white wine
   Index)   dash each of salt and pepper
              1 tablespoon chives

Put chicken breasts in a frying pan and add just enough water to cover. Simmer 30 minutes. Let cool in broth. Remove skin and bones from chicken, keeping the meat mainly in two pieces. Put chicken meat into a shallow casserole. Combine the Béchamel, sour cream, wine, salt, and pepper. Pour over the chicken. Put in 350° oven for 20 minutes or until heated through. Garnish with chives, and serve.

DUCK À L'ORANGE

½ duck (about 4-pound duck)   1 cup chicken bouillon
3 tablespoons butter   ⅓ cup dry white wine
salt and pepper   3 oranges

Ask butcher to saw the duck in half lengthwise, down the center of front and back. Wrap one half of the duck very well and freeze for later use.

Clean the other half of the duck well, wash, and pat dry. Heat butter in a large pan or Dutch oven. Brown duck well on all sides over medium heat. Sprinkle with salt and pepper and add the bouillon, wine, and the juice of 2 of the oranges. Add also the giblets from the duck if you wish. Cover and simmer for 2 hours, adding more liquid if necessary to keep duck moist. (*Simmer; don't boil.*)

Remove duck from pan. Strain the juices and return them to the pan. Add the rind of the third orange (use potato peeler to peel off just the colored part). Squeeze juice from orange and add to the sauce. Boil 2 minutes. Put duck on serving plate or platter. Pour the hot sauce over. Serve with hot brown, white, or wild rice, or a combination of the three.

To serve four: Cook the whole duck as directed, but double remaining ingredients.

To serve six: Choose a 6-pound duck and cook the same way, doubling the other ingredients.

*ROASTED CORNISH GAME HEN

2 Cornish game hens (1 per   salt and pepper
  person)   2 teaspoons butter
              melted butter for basting

If game hens are frozen, thaw without unwrapping, at refrigerator temperature, for 24 hours. Remove from wrapper, wash, and pat dry. Season cavity of each hen with salt and pepper. Add a teaspoon of butter to each. Tuck wingtips behind shoulders, and place birds on a shallow baking pan, leaving several inches of space between them. Roast in a moderate oven (350°) for about 1 hour or until leg joint moves easily. Baste occasionally with melted butter while roasting.

Note: You can add a seasoning to the melted butter such as curry powder, chili powder, prepared or dry mustard, lemon juice, parsley, tarragon, basil, oregano, or sage—just a pinch for subtle flavoring, about ¼ teaspoon for a stronger flavor.

*SPIT-ROASTED, CASHEW-STUFFED PHEASANT

1 young pheasant (about 1 to 2   2 tablespoons butter
   pounds)   ½ teaspoon salt
1 cup chopped cashews   dash of pepper
1 cup chicken broth   3 slices bacon, uncooked
4 slices bacon, cooked crisp,
   drained, crumbled

Carefully wipe the inside of the pheasant with paper toweling. Simmer the cashews in the broth until liquid is absorbed and cashews are tender. Mix in the cooked bacon, butter, salt, and pepper. Use this mixture to stuff the pheasant. Skewer to close the opening. Tie the uncooled bacon over the breast of the bird with heavy cotton cord. Put bird on spit and roast over medium-hot coals for 1 hour. To serve, cut bird in half with kitchen or poultry shears, cutting down the back and breastbone. Divide the stuffing between the two servings.

Note: This stuffing and cooking procedure works well with Cornish game hen, too.

*CORNISH GAME HEN WITH WILD RICE

2 Cornish game hens   4-ounce can chopped
4 tablespoons butter   mushrooms, with liquid
½ cup uncooked wild rice   1½ cups chicken broth
               2 tablespoons cognac or brandy

Brown the game hen in the butter in frying pan over medium-
high heat until it is golden all over. Meanwhile, put the wild
rice, mushrooms, and chicken broth into a casserole. When the
hens are golden, place them on top of the rice mixture. Pour pan
drippings on top. Cover tightly and bake in a moderate oven
(350°) for 45 minutes or until the rice is cooked. (If liquid
evaporates before the rice is soft, add water to the dish.) Spoon
the cognac over the game hens and ignite. When flames ex-
tinguish themselves, serve.

*BROILED CORNISH GAME HEN

This is so simple and good!

2 Cornish game hens, split in   2 tablespoons lemon juice
   half lengthwise   ¼ teaspoon salt
¼ cup melted butter   freshly ground pepper

Wash Cornish hens and wipe them dry. Lay the halves on the
broiler pan with cut side up. Brush with mixture of melted butter,
lemon juice, and salt. Broil about 8 inches from source of heat
for 15 minutes, brushing occasionally with the butter mixture.
Turn them over, brush with more butter, and broil for 15 minutes
more or until the juices from the meat run clear. Grind pepper
over the halves, spoon on some of the pan juices, and serve 2
pieces to each diner.

*RICE-STUFFED CORNISH GAME HEN

¾ cup cooked wild rice or
   brown rice
2 tablespoons buttered, toasted
   bread crumbs
¼ cup chopped pecans or
   filberts

1 tablespoon cream
1 egg, slightly beaten
salt
2 Rock Cornish game hens or
   small game birds

melted butter

Combine the rice, crumbs, nuts, cream, and egg. Taste; then add salt. Stuff the birds with the mixture and skewer shut. Brush outsides with butter. Bake in a hot oven (450°) for 10 minutes; reduce heat to 350°, and roast about 30 minutes more or until leg moves easily.

Rice, Wild Rice,
Bulgur Wheat, and Pasta

These are the dishes that add class to a meal. Serve them in place of potatoes as a starch element. They are especially suitable for cooking for two because they can be cooked in small amounts.

Be sure to follow the basic directions for cooking rice and wild rice, even if these ingredients are to be used in another dish, such as a casserole.

Recipes that can be doubled or tripled without further instructions are marked with an asterisk (*).

RICE (*Basic Cooking Directions*)

1 cup regular rice, short or long grain

2 cups liquid—water, bouillon, or juice

1 teaspoon salt

Combine rice, liquid, and salt in a 3-quart saucepan that has a tight-fitting cover. Bring to a boil and stir enough to separate the rice grains. Lower heat to simmering. Cover pan and cook rice 15 minutes without removing lid or stirring. If rice is not yet tender, replace cover and cook 2 to 6 minutes longer. Remove from heat and from cooking pan. Fluff with fork. Makes 3 cups cooked rice.

FOR FLUFFY RICE

Let rice stand in the covered pan for 5 to 10 minutes longer, to steam dry. Fluff with a fork.

FOR TENDER RICE

Add ⅓ cup more liquid to the rice, and increase cooking time 5 minutes.

FEATHERED RICE

This is great with steak or anything barbecued.

½ cup long-grain rice
½ cup sliced fresh mushrooms
½ small onion, diced
2 tablespoons butter
1¼ cups chicken bouillon or
  water

1 teaspoon salt (if you are using
  water for liquid; omit if
  using bouillon that is salty)

Put unwashed rice on a cookie sheet and roast uncovered in moderate oven (350°) until it is golden brown—about 10 minutes. Meanwhile, sauté the mushrooms and onion in the butter for 5 minutes. Put rice into a 1-quart casserole with a cover, and add the sautéed mushrooms and onion plus liquid and salt. Stir well. Cover tightly and bake in a moderate oven (350°) for 35 minutes. Do not open the dish while cooking or valuable steam will escape, leaving the rice on the dry side.

To serve four: Double the quantities—the 1-quart casserole will still be sufficient.

To serve six: Triple the quantities, but use a 1½-quart casserole.

*BASIC RICE PILAF

1 tablespoon butter   ⅓ cup long-grain rice
                      ⅔ cup hot bouillon

Heat butter in a heavy casserole or pan with a lid. Add the rice and stir until it is heated and becomes whitish in color. Add the hot bouillon; bring to a boil, reduce heat to very low, cover, and simmer for 15 minutes. Do not peek or stir. This yields 1 cup cooked Rice Pilaf, a very basic pilaf to which you can add various things.

RICE PILAF WITH VEGETABLES

Prepare Basic Rice Pilaf as directed in the preceding recipe. For each 2 servings add 1 cup diced cooked vegetables, such as mixed vegetables, peas, corn, or green beans cut in ½-inch pieces.

RICE PILAF WITH MEAT

Prepare Basic Rice Pilaf as in the first pilaf recipe. For each 2 servings add 1 to 2 cups diced leftover cooked meat, poultry, or ham. You can also add cooked vegetables and an additional pat of butter.

BASQUE PILAF

Prepare Basic Rice Pilaf as directed in the first pilaf recipe, with these additions: 1 chopped small onion, 1 chopped small red pepper, a pinch of saffron, and 1 teaspoon turmeric (all added to the butter and rice). Then add the liquid and cook until rice is tender. When rice is cooked, add 2 cups diced cooked pork, 1 cup cooked peas, ¼ cup dry white wine, and 1 cup diced cooked lobster or shrimp. Heat through before serving.

RICE PILAF AMANDINE

Prepare Basic Rice Pilaf, and turn hot rice into a baking dish. Dot liberally with butter and stir it into the rice. Top with ½ cup slivered almonds and bake in a hot oven (400°) for 10 minutes or until almonds are browned.

CURRIED RICE PILAF

Prepare Basic Rice Pilaf, but add 1 teaspoon curry powder to liquid before adding it to the rice.

RICE PILAF NANCY

Prepare Basic Rice Pilaf. Soak 2 tablespoons seedless raisins in water for 5 minutes. Brown ½ pound Polish sausages (cut in ½-inch pieces) in frying pan without additional fat. Add 1 large banana, sliced, along with the raisins. Add the rice, folding all together carefully. Cover and cook until rice is very hot.

*BASIC WHEAT PILAF

Cracked wheat made of wheat grown in the United States is almost identical to the bulgur of Middle Eastern countries. You can do almost the same things with cooked cracked wheat as you can do with rice. Buttered and cooked just to the point where it still has texture and is not mushy, it is an excellent accompaniment to meats. Combine it with wild rice or regular or brown rice and nuts and vegetables, or use it as a base for casseroles.

½ cup quick-cooking cracked wheat
1 tablespoon butter or bacon drippings
1 small onion, chopped, or 1 teaspoon instant onion
¼ teaspoon salt
¾ cup chicken stock or broth

Sauté the wheat in the butter or bacon drippings; add the onion and cook 5 minutes. Add salt and chicken broth, and let it simmer, covered, until liquid is absorbed (15 to 20 minutes)—wheat should be crunchy. If you prefer it less so, add ¼ cup more liquid.

*PILAF WITH CLAM JUICE

Drain liquid from 1 can (about 7 ounces) of minced clams. Add enough water to equal ¾ cup liquid, and ⅛ teaspoon thyme. Cook as directed for Basic Wheat Pilaf—until pilaf is crunchy. Fold in the clams, heat through, and serve.

*MUSHROOM-TOMATO PILAF

Drain the juice from a 3- or 4-ounce can of chopped mushrooms and measure; add enough tomato juice to make ¾ cup liquid. Use this liquid in place of the chicken broth to cook Basic Wheat Pilaf. When it is cooked, fold in the mushrooms and ¼ teaspoon basil, a dash of sugar and a peeled and chopped tomato. Heat through, and serve.

*WATER CHESTNUT–SOY SAUCE PILAF

Omit the salt in recipe for Basic Wheat Pilaf, and for the liquid use 1 tablespoon soy sauce and enough beef bouillon to equal ¾ cup. When pilaf is cooked, stir in a 5-ounce can of water chestnuts, drained and sliced. Heat through and serve.

WILD RICE (*Basic Cooking Directions*)

Wild rice is like gold. Even in amounts for two, its price is fairly formidable, but its earthy, nutty flavor is worth the expense. Try it once just for a treat. You can freeze any amount of cooked wild rice that is left over, and in the following recipes you can combine it with long-grain or brown rice according to your taste, although the recipes given are for just straight wild rice.

⅓ cup uncooked wild rice   ¼ teaspoon salt
1 cup cold water

Wash rice well and drain it. Put it into a pan with the cold water and salt. Cover, and bring to a boil. Remove cover and continue boiling without stirring until rice is tender, about 30 minutes. If necessary, add more water to pan.

Because wild rice is a natural wild product—that is, not cultivated by man—it is not consistent in its cooking time. It varies, often greatly. The growing season and the method of harvest have much to do with this. So don't fret if it is not done in 30 minutes; simply add more water and continue to cook the precious stuff until it is tender. Overnight soaking is sometimes recommended, but I have not found that necessary.

This amount makes 1 cup of cooked wild rice. For larger amounts, increase the ingredients proportionately.

BAKED WILD RICE PILAF

⅓ cup wild rice   1 cup chicken broth or beef
                                        bouillon

Rinse wild rice with water and drain well. Put into a casserole that has a cover. Pour the bouillon over the rice, and put on the cover. Bake in a moderately hot oven (375°) for one hour, or until rice absorbs all the liquid and is tender.

To serve four: Use ½ cup wild rice and 1½ cups bouillon.

To serve six: Use ⅔ cup wild rice and 2 cups bouillon.

WILD RICE WITH PEAS

Prepare wild rice according to the basic cooking directions. Add 1 cup cooked fresh or frozen green peas, and heat through before serving.

WILD RICE AMANDINE

Prepare wild rice according to the basic cooking directions. Meanwhile, sauté ¼ cup slivered almonds in 2 tablespoons butter until they are golden. Just before serving, top the wild rice with the almonds.

WILD RICE WITH ONIONS

Prepare wild rice according to the basic cooking directions. Drain an 8-ounce can of white onions and heat them in 2 tablespoons of butter for 5 minutes over low heat. Add to the rice before serving.

*PARSLIED WILD RICE

1 cup cooked wild rice	3 tablespoons chopped fresh
salt	parsley
freshly ground pepper	3 tablespoons grated Parmesan
2 tablespoons butter	cheese

Cook wild rice according to the basic directions. Add salt and pepper to taste. Blend in the butter and fresh parsley. Turn into heated serving dish and sprinkle with the Parmesan. Serve immediately.

*WILD RICE WITH MUSHROOMS

1 cup cooked wild rice	¼ teaspoon salt
2 tablespoons butter	freshly ground pepper
1 green onion, chopped	dash of nutmeg
¼ pound fresh mushrooms, sliced	

Cook wild rice according to basic cooking directions, and have it ready. Melt butter in frying pan, and add the onion and mushrooms. Cook, stirring carefully, for 3 minutes. Season with salt, pepper, and nutmeg. Add the cooked, drained wild rice. Keep hot until serving time.

*TARRAGON BUTTERED NOODLES

4 ounces noodles   2 tablespoons butter
pinch of tarragon   ¼ cup heavy cream
                  salt and pepper to taste

Cook the noodles as directed on the package, until tender but not mushy. Drain well. Combine the tarragon and butter in a pan; heat until butter is melted. Add the cooked, drained noodles, and stir. Pour the cream over; taste, and add salt and pepper. Heat through and serve immediately. (The noodles can be cooked in advance and reheated in the butter at serving time, if desired.)

*NOODLES AU GRATIN

4 ounces egg noodles   3 tablespoons butter
¼ cup each shredded jack or   dash nutmeg
    white brick cheese and grated   ¼ cup heavy cream
    Parmesan   salt and pepper to taste

Cook the noodles as directed on the package, and drain. They should be tender but not soft. Combine the cheeses, and sprinkle a third of the mixture in the bottoms of two individual-size casseroles or *au gratin* dishes, or a 1-quart casserole. Melt butter in a frying pan; add the drained noodles, another third of the cheese, the nutmeg, cream, and salt and pepper to taste. Turn noodle mixture into the baking dish or dishes. Top with remaining cheese, and brown in a hot oven (400°) for 10 minutes.

*NOODLES À L'ITALIENNE

Use the same ingredients as in the preceding recipe, but combine all in a frying pan with the entire amount of cheese added at one time. Toss over medium heat until noodles are hot, and serve immediately.

*BASIL BUTTERED NOODLES

½ package (6-ounce size) egg   1 tablespoon salt
   noodles, any width   2 tablespoons butter
1 to 2 quarts boiling water .   ½ teaspoon basil

Cook noodles in boiling salted water until tender (8 to 10 minutes). Drain; rinse with hot water. Melt butter, add the basil, then the drained noodles. Toss until well mixed. Serve at once.

*PINCHED NOODLES

½ cup sifted flour   1 egg
¼ teaspoon salt   boiling salted water

Sift the flour and salt together into a bowl. Add egg and mix until a stiff dough forms. Knead until smooth. Roll out to ¼ inch thickness on a board. Pinch off pieces about the size of marbles, drop them into boiling salted water, and cook 15 minutes. Drain. Keep it hot until ready to serve. Serve with melted butter.

*MUSHROOM MACARONI IN PORT

Here's an elegant twist to macaroni. Bring it right into the candlelight!

4 ounces elbow macaroni (about   ¼ pound mushrooms, chopped
   1½ cups)   3 tablespoons butter, melted
¾ cup shredded Gruyère, brick,   1 cup port
   or jack cheese .   salt and pepper to taste

Cook the macaroni in a large amount of boiling water (salted) according to directions on the package. Macaroni should be tender but not mushy. Drain. Put half the macaroni into a well-buttered 1-quart casserole. Top with half the cheese and all the mushrooms. Sprinkle with salt and pepper. Cover with remaining macaroni and top with remaining cheese. Drizzle the melted butter over, and pour the port over all. Bake for 20 minutes in a hot oven (400°).

*MACARONI WITH COTTAGE CHEESE

This is an excellent accompaniment to barbecued meats or poultry done with a spicy sauce.

4 ounces elbow macaroni	1 cup creamed cottage cheese,
boiling salted water	small or large curd
2 tablespoons melted butter	dash of salt
2 tablespoons grated Parmesan cheese	

Cook the macaroni in boiling salted water as directed on the package until *al dente*, or tender but not soft. Drain and mix with the butter, cottage cheese, and salt. Turn into heated serving dish and top with the Parmesan, preferably freshly grated.

*SPAGHETTI WITH CLAM SAUCE

Serve this either as a first course or as the main course for a light meal.

2 tablespoons salad oil or olive oil	8-ounce can tomato sauce
⅛ teaspoon garlic powder	2 tablespoons tomato paste
1 small onion, chopped	2 tablespoons minced parsley
7-ounce can minced clams	4 ounces spaghetti
	boiling salted water
freshly grated Parmesan cheese	

Heat the oil, garlic powder, onion, and the juice from the clams in a pan. Add the tomato sauce and paste, and the parsley. Simmer for 15 to 20 minutes while the spaghetti is cooking in boiling salted water, according to package directions. Drain and mix with the clam sauce and clams. Serve piping hot, and pass a bowl of freshly grated Parmesan cheese.

Vegetables

Vegetables too often get lost in the shuffle—and are given secondary consideration when it comes to meal planning. Both the variety they can add to a meal and their nutritional value are greatly underestimated.

Frozen vegetables are plentiful the year round, and convenient, but whenever possible, treat yourself to fresh vegetables. Select them for quality; carefully check the color and maturity of such things as green beans and corn. Fresh vegetables have an added advantage in that they can be bought in the small quantity appropriate for two. However, when using frozen vegetables, you can cut a package in half quite readily with a serrated knife. The unneeded portion should, of course, immediately be wrapped so that it is airtight and returned to the freezer.

Experiment freely with herbs and spices when cooking vegetables. They blend beautifully, and will add variety to old favorites. Try green beans with tarragon, dill, basil, or sage. Try peas with mint, dill, or a pinch of allspice. Try spinach with a pinch of nutmeg!

Recipes in this chapter that can be doubled or tripled without further instruction are marked with an asterisk (*).

*ARTICHOKES WITH TARTAR SAUCE

Prepare as for artichokes with Horseradish–Sour Cream Sauce, but fill and serve with Tartar Sauce (see Index).

154

ARTICHOKES (*Basic Cooking Directions*)

2 artichokes

Cut off stalks, pull off hard outer leaves, and trim off points of remaining leaves with scissors. Cut off about ⅓ of the top, thus removing many thorny-ended leaves. Put artichokes into pan of boiling salted water. Cook 20 to 25 minutes for medium-sized artichokes, or until base is tender but not mushy. Drain cooked artichokes by turning them upside down to let water run out from between the leaves. Serve hot with melted butter as a dip, or cold, or as suggested in the next several recipes.

To eat an artichoke, remove leaves one by one, dip in butter (if desired), and with your teeth scrape off the meaty portion from the bottom of each leaf. The leaves are meatier toward the center of the artichoke. The "choke" portion in the very center can be removed before serving or at the table; use a knife or spoon to scrape this dry, bristly portion out. The heart of the artichoke, the soft meaty base that remains after the leaves are removed, is the tastiest part—the "fillet" of the artichoke. Serve 1 artichoke per person.

*ARTICHOKES WITH HORSERADISH–SOUR CREAM SAUCE

2 artichokes   ½ cup Horseradish–Sour
salt   Cream Sauce (see Index)

Trim, cook, cool, and drain artichokes as explained in the basic cooking directions. Scoop out choke with a spoon. Sprinkle each artichoke with salt. Fill with the Horseradish–Sour Cream Sauce. Chill before serving time.

*ARTICHOKES WITH VINAIGRETTE

Prepare as in the preceding recipe, but fill and serve with Vinaigrette Sauce (see Index).

*ARTICHOKES WITH MAYONNAISE

2 artichokes   ½ cup freshly made Mayonnaise
lemon juice   (see Index)
salt

Trim, cook, and cool the artichokes, and drain thoroughly, according to the instructions given in the basic cooking directions. Scoop out the choke from the center of each, leaving a "cup" for the mayonnaise. Sprinkle with lemon juice and salt, and fill with mayonnaise. Chill thoroughly before serving.

*ARTICHOKES WITH HOT HOLLANDAISE SAUCE

2 artichokes   ½ cup Hollandaise Sauce (see
boiling water   Index)

Trim as directed in the basic cooking directions, and cook artichokes for 5 minutes in boiling water. Remove, drain, and scoop out choke. Return to water and cook for 15 minutes more, or until hearts of artichokes are tender. Drain. Fill centers with sauce, and serve immediately.

*ARTICHOKES WITH HOT BUTTER SAUCE

Prepare artichokes as for serving with hot Hollandaise Sauce, as in the preceding recipe, but fill centers with melted butter.

*ARTICHOKES WITH MOUSSELINE SAUCE

Prepare artichokes as for serving with hot Hollandaise Sauce, but fill centers with hot Mousseline Sauce (see Index).

*CARROTS TARRAGON

½ bunch carrots   ½ teaspoon sugar
water   dash of salt
1 tablespoon butter   1 teaspoon tarragon leaves
          1 teaspoon chopped parsley

   Peel carrots and cut into 1-inch pieces. Cook in just enough
water to cover for 10 minutes or until carrots are tender-crisp.
Drain. Add butter, sugar, salt, tarragon, and parsley to hot carrots.
Toss until ingredients coat carrots evenly. Serve hot.

*GLAZED CARROTS

2 medium-sized carrots   1½ teaspoons sugar
¼ cup water   pinch of salt
1 tablespoon butter   parsley

   Scrape the carrots and slice them very thin. Put in a pan, cover
with the water, and add butter, sugar, and salt. Simmer, covered,
over low to medium heat until all liquid has cooked away and
carrots are tender. Shake pan constantly as liquid becomes low, to
glaze the carrots. Sprinkle with parsley to garnish.

*GREEN BEANS WITH GARLIC

1 cup cooked green beans   ¼ cup sour cream
          ½ small clove garlic, mashed

Place hot cooked beans on a serving plate. Combine the sour cream
and garlic, and spoon over the beans. Serve immediately.

*GREEN BEANS SAUTÉED IN BUTTER

½ pound green beans   2 tablespoons butter
3 tablespoons water   chopped parsley
                salt and pepper to taste

Trim stems from beans, and cut bean into 2-inch pieces. Put beans and water in covered pan, and cook over high heat for 5 minutes. Remove cover. Drain off any liquid. Add butter and parsley, and cook and stir 2 to 3 minutes more. Add salt and pepper to taste.

*GREEN BEANS IN CREAM

½ pound green beans, whole   1 tablespoon butter
water   ⅓ cup heavy cream
                salt and pepper

Wash beans and trim off stems. Put whole beans in pan and add about a half-inch of water. Bring to a boil and cook 5 minutes. Drain well. Add butter, and toss to coat the beans. Add cream. Bring to a boil and cook until cream is reduced to half the original amount. Add salt and pepper to taste. Serve hot.

*GREEN BEANS IN BROWNED BUTTER

½ pound fresh green beans, cut   3 tablespoons butter
    into 2-inch pieces   parsley
boiling salted water   salt and pepper

Remove stem ends from beans. Cook beans in small amount of boiling salted water for 8 to 10 minutes or until they are tender-crisp. Drain. Put on a serving dish. Melt butter in pan and heat until browned, but not burned; then pour it over the beans. Sprinkle with parsley. Season with salt and pepper.

*GREEN BEANS AMANDINE

Prepare Green Beans Browned in Butter, but with the butter add ¼ cup slivered almonds.

*GREEN BEANS AND BACON

½ pound fresh green beans cut into 1½-inch lengths, stems and tips removed	2 tablespoons salad oil
	2 tablespoons catsup
	1 tablespoon vinegar
½ teaspoon salt	2 radishes, quartered
dash of pepper	2 slices crisp cooked bacon

Cook beans in boiling salted water until they are tender. Drain. Mix together the salt, pepper, oil, catsup, and vinegar. Pour mixture over the hot drained beans and add the radishes; toss lightly. Crumble bacon on top, and serve hot.

*GREEN BEANS WITH LEMON SAUCE

½ pound green beans, cut in 1½-inch lengths, stems and tips removed	⅛ teaspoon salt
	dash of pepper
	1 tablespoon minced fresh parsley
1 tablespoon melted butter	

juice of ½ lemon

Cook beans in a small amount of salted water until they are tender-crisp. Drain and put in a serving dish. Mix the butter, salt, pepper, parsley, and lemon juice, and pour over the beans. Serve hot.

*GREEN BEANS AU GRATIN

Prepare Green Beans in Cream (preceding recipe). Put into a casserole, pouring all the sauce over. Sprinkle with 3 tablespoons Parmesan cheese. Brown under broiler for about 2 minutes.

*LIMA BEANS WITH ONION

1 cup cooked lima beans   1 green onion, chopped
¼ cup sour cream

Put hot cooked lima beans in a hot serving dish. Spoon sour cream on top and sprinkle with the green onion. Serve immediately. Quick and easy!

*SAUTÉED ONIONS (*to go with steak*)

1 large onion, peeled   2 whole cloves
2 tablespoons butter   ¼ teaspoon salt
                ¼ cup red Burgundy

Slice the onion about ¼ inch thick, to make rings. Heat butter in pan. Add onion and whole cloves, and cook, stirring, until onion is golden in color. Remove onion rings to a serving plate and sprinkle with salt. Add Burgundy to pan, bring to a boil, and cook, scraping pan well, until liquid is reduced by half. Pour liquid over the onions and serve hot.

*TROPICAL TOMATOES

1 large tomato   salt and paprika
1 small firm green-tipped   1½ tablespoons finely shredded
  banana   Cheddar cheese

Remove stem end from tomato, and cut tomato into 4 slices crosswise. Peel banana, and cut into thin slices. Put tomato slices onto a heatproof platter. Top with overlapping circles of banana slices. Sprinkle with salt, paprika, and grated cheese. Broil about 5 inches from heat until cheese is melted and tomatoes are slightly cooked, about 10 minutes. Serve immediately.

CAULIFLOWER À L'ITALIENNE

½ head cauliflower	½ cup shredded brick or
boiling salted water	Gruyère cheese
juice of ½ lemon	pinch of oregano
3 tablespoons soft butter	salt and pepper

Trim the cauliflower and separate the flowerets. Add them to boiling salted water along with the lemon juice. Cook 20 minutes and drain thoroughly. Transfer to buttered casserole or 2 individual casserole dishes (the size of small foil pie pans). Spread with the butter; sprinkle with cheese, oregano, salt, and pepper. Bake in a hot oven (400°) for 10 minutes, or broil about 6 inches from heat until cheese is melted.

To serve four: Double all quantities.

To serve six: Triple all quantities. For this number, you will need a very large head of cauliflower or 1½ smaller heads, according to what is available.

BUTTER-STEAMED CELERY

We often forget that celery by itself is a delightful vegetable. Here's my favorite way of preparing it. The garnish of bacon crumbles can be the new high-protein bacon bits available in a jar. They add color, flavor, and texture to this dish.

1 tablespoon butter	2 tablespoons water
1 cup thinly sliced celery, cut	salt and pepper to taste
diagonally	1 tablespoon bacon crumbles

Heat the butter in a frying pan and add the celery. Stir and fry about a half minute or until the celery is heated through. Add the water, and cover. Cook over medium heat for 2 minutes. Add salt and pepper to taste, and sprinkle with the bacon crumbles.

*FENNEL WITH CREAM

Fennel is a plant of Italian origin. Every so often, at least in the Middle West, it appears in the market. Many people pass it by because they don't know what to do with it. Fennel has a mild licorice-like flavor, and is somewhat like celery in appearance. It has a fleshy, bulbous stem, with long leaves shooting up from it. All parts are edible.

1 whole head fennel   2 tablespoons water
2 tablespoons butter   4 tablespoons heavy cream
                        salt and pepper to taste

Prepare the fennel for cooking—wash well, separate the leaves, and cut the fleshy part into thin slices. Heat the butter in a pan. Add the fennel all at once, and stir over medium heat for about a half-minute. Add the water, cover, and steam for 2 to 3 minutes, or until the fennel is tender-crisp. Add the heavy cream and bring to boil over high heat, tossing fennel and cream together until well blended. Add salt and pepper to taste.

*BAKED EGGPLANT, ITALIAN STYLE

This is my own favorite way with eggplant. The flavor of the marinade permeates the otherwise rather bland vegetable, and it is tender and juicy.

1 small eggplant, or ½ large   4 tablespoons olive oil or
    eggplant   salad oil
½ clove garlic, mashed   1 tablespoon vinegar or lemon
1 teaspoon salt   juice
pinch of oregano

Peel eggplant and cut into 4 thick wedges. Combine the garlic, salt, oregano, oil, and vinegar into a sauce, and brush all of it onto the eggplant wedges. Place them on a baking sheet and bake in a hot oven (450°) for 20 minutes, brushing twice with the drippings during cooking. Serve hot.

*PEAS ITALIANO

If you keep a package of croutons handy, you can use them to garnish buttered cooked vegetables, whether canned or frozen. In this recipe they add texture to cooked peas.

1 tablespoon butter
2 tablespoons packaged crisp
    croutons
pinch *each* of oregano and
    basil

1 tablespoon grated Parmesan
    cheese
1 cup hot cooked peas

Melt the butter in a pan and add the croutons. Add the oregano, basil, and Parmesan cheese; toss lightly. Just before serving, blend with the hot cooked peas.

*BEETS WITH MUSTARD BUTTER

2 tablespoons soft butter
1 teaspoon prepared mustard

1 teaspoon vinegar
pinch of tarragon

1 cup cooked beets, diced

Blend the butter, mustard, vinegar, and tarragon. Heat the beets. Add the mustard butter, mix lightly, and serve.

*CRISP-TOPPED CORN

1 tablespoon butter
¼ cup herb-seasoned packaged
    stuffing mix

1 cup hot whole kernel corn,
    canned or frozen, thawed

Melt the butter in a pan and add the stuffing mix. Stir over medium heat until it is crisp and lightly browned. Sprinkle over the hot cooked corn.

*ASPARAGUS WITH DILL SAUCE

¾ pound fresh asparagus   ¼ teaspoon dillweed
½ cup sour cream   dash of salt or more to taste

Cook the asparagus until it is tender-crisp in a small amount of water (about 8 to 10 minutes). Mix the sour cream with the dillweed to make the sauce. Spoon it over the asparagus, and sprinkle lightly with salt. Serve immediately.

*GREEN OR WHITE ASPARAGUS WITH BUTTER

10-ounce package frozen   salted water
 asparagus or ½ pound fresh   3 tablespoons melted butter
 green or white asparagus   salt and pepper

Cook frozen asparagus as directed on the package, or cook fresh asparagus in a half-inch of boiling salted water until they are tender-crisp—about 10 minutes. Drain. Serve with melted butter drizzled over. Add salt and pepper to taste.

*ASPARAGUS AU GRATIN

10-ounce package frozen   2 tablespoons grated Parmesan
 asparagus or ½ pound fresh   cheese
½ cup Mornay Sauce (see   2 tablespoons melted butter
 Index)

Cook frozen asparagus as directed on the package, or cook fresh asparagus in a half-inch of water until they are tender-crisp. Drain. Arrange in small casserole. Pour sauce over evenly. Sprinkle with the cheese and melted butter. Place under the broiler for 1 to 2 minutes or until lightly browned.

ASPARAGUS À LA FLAMANDE

10-ounce package frozen
   asparagus or ½ pound fresh
3 tablespoons butter

1 hard-cooked egg, pressed
   through sieve
salt and pepper

Cook frozen asparagus as directed on the package, or cook fresh asparagus in about a half-inch of water for 10 minutes or until they are tender-crisp. Drain. Put on a serving dish. Pour melted butter on top and garnish with egg. Serve, and add salt and pepper to taste.

To serve four or six: Use 2 packages of frozen asparagus or 1 to 1½ pounds fresh.

*BRUSSELS SPROUTS AND WILD RICE

What a flavorsome combination this is! It is an excellent accompaniment to barbecued, broiled, or roasted meat—only a salad and bread need be added to make a memorable meal.

1 package (10 to 12 ounces)
   frozen Brussels sprouts,
   thawed, or ¾ pound fresh
water

2 tablespoons butter
dash of garlic salt
1 cup cooked wild rice
   (see Index)

Put the Brussels sprouts into a pan; add enough water just to cover the first layer. Bring to a boil, covered, and cook for 8 to 10 minutes, or until sprouts are tender-crisp. Drain thoroughly. (If using frozen sprouts, follow the package directions.) Chop coarsely. Melt the butter in the same cooking pan, and add the chopped sprouts, the garlic salt, and wild rice. Season to taste with salt and pepper, heat through, and serve.

*CURRIED BRUSSELS SPROUTS

1 pound fresh, or 11-ounce
  package frozen, Brussels
  sprouts

½ cup heavy cream
1 teaspoon curry powder
salt and pepper

Trim the sprouts and remove heavy stems and yellow outer leaves. Put in pan with water and boil 20 minutes. (If using frozen sprouts, cook according to package directions.) Drain thoroughly. Chop fine. Put in pan with cream and curry powder. Season to taste with salt and pepper. Cook until sprouts have absorbed most of the cream, stirring constantly. Serve immediately.

*MIXED VEGETABLE MEDLEY

Frozen mixed vegetables are so colorful that they need only be cooked, buttered, and seasoned with a pinch of herb to make them presentable for the table. Buy them in the large bags, and you can measure out the amount you need, seal the remainder, and store it in the freezer. Usually, I find the 10- to 12-ounce packages of frozen are a little too much for two servings.

This recipe calls for no liquid because generally there's enough frost on the vegetables to create steam. However, if you feel it is necessary to add water, use just a couple of tablespoons.

3 tablespoons butter
1 small clove garlic, minced
¼ cup chopped green onion
1 medium-sized potato, peeled
  and diced in ½-inch cubes

1 cup frozen mixed vegetables
salt and pepper to taste
½ teaspoon tarragon

Heat butter in a heavy frying pan. Add the garlic, onion, and potato, and sauté, stirring, until the potato is lightly browned. Add the mixed vegetables, cover, and cook over low heat, stirring occasionally, until the vegetables are tender, about 5 minutes. Add the salt, pepper, and tarragon.

*PEAS WITH GREEN GRAPES

Green seedless grapes add a quick gourmet touch to green peas whether the peas are canned, frozen, or fresh. This combination is especially nice with fish or chicken.

1 cup cooked green peas   ½ cup small seedless green
  (8-ounce can of peas,   grapes
  drained, or cooked frozen or   1 tablespoon butter
  fresh peas)   salt and pepper to taste
           pinch of dried tarragon

Combine the green peas and the green grapes. Heat the butter in a pan, add the peas and grapes, and stir over medium-high heat until they are just heated through. Add salt and pepper to taste, and the pinch of tarragon.

MUSHROOMS ON TOAST

Keep this recipe in mind for an excellent little meal or snack.

¼ pound fresh mushrooms   2 tablespoons minced parsley
lemon juice   ⅛ teaspoon salt
1 clove garlic, mashed   freshly ground pepper
  (optional)   2 slices buttered toasted French
2 tablespoons butter   bread

Wash the mushrooms, dry, and cut in quarters. Sprinkle with lemon juice. In a small frying pan heat the garlic and butter. Add the mushrooms, and cook until they have lost their whiteness but still have texture, about 3 minutes. Stir in the parsley, and sprinkle with salt and pepper. Keep hot until serving time. Divide mushrooms between the two slices of bread, and serve.

To serve four: Double all quantities except garlic; use just 1 clove.

To serve six: Triple all quantities except garlic; use just 1 clove.

GARLIC MUSHROOMS

¼ pound whole mushrooms   1 small clove garlic, mashed
2 tablespoons lemon juice   1 tablespoon butter
1 cup water   ½ teaspoon basil

Choose firm white mushrooms, not very large in size. Wash well. Put lemon juice and water into pan. Bring to a boil and add the mushrooms; cook 3 minutes. Drain off water. Add the garlic, butter, and basil to the mushrooms, and stir over low heat until mushrooms are well coated with butter and basil. Serve over broiled steak or with a roast.

For four servings: Double all quantities except garlic.

For six servings: Triple all quantities except garlic; use just 1 clove.

*BROILED MUSHROOMS

¼ pound fresh mushrooms   olive oil or melted butter
1 cup water   salt
1 tablespoon lemon juice   freshly ground pepper

Choose firm white mushrooms. Soak 5 minutes in a mixture of the water and lemon juice. Drain. Dip each one in oil or butter. Sprinkle with salt and pepper and place on a broiling rack. Broil 7 or 8 inches from the source of heat, turning once, for about 8 minutes or until mushrooms are lightly browned. (You can broil them over the charcoal grill if you're grilling steaks. In that case, the mushrooms are easier to handle if put on skewers.) Serve hot.

*SPINACH WITH NUTMEG

This vegetable is great with a broiled steak!

1 cup cooked chopped spinach   ¼ cup sour cream
                    dash of nutmeg

Drain spinach of all the water possible. Blend in the sour cream and nutmeg, and heat to serving temperature but don't boil. Add salt and pepper to taste, and serve immediately.

*SPINACH WITH MUSHROOMS

½ pound fresh spinach, well   1½ tablespoons butter
   washed   ¼ teaspoon salt
⅛ pound fresh mushrooms   2 tablespoons grated Parmesan
   (approximately)   cheese

Cook spinach in a small amount of water until tender (about 5 minutes). Drain and chop. Chop all but 2 mushroom caps (save those for garnish). Heat butter in pan; add the mushrooms, including the two whole caps. Cook, stirring, over high heat for 2 minutes. Add the salt. Remove the whole caps. Combine chopped mushrooms with spinach and Parmesan cheese. Keep hot until ready to serve. Garnish each serving with a mushroom cap.

*SUMMER SQUASH SAUTÉ

2 small yellow summer squash   salt and pepper to taste
2 tablespoons *each* butter   pinch of basil
   and water   2 to 3 tablespoons light cream

Scrub the squash well and slice them ¼ inch thick. Heat the butter in a pan and add the squash; add the water and stir and fry until the squash is hot and about half cooked (2 to 3 minutes). Add salt and pepper, basil, and the cream. Cover and hold over low heat for 5 minutes or until ready to serve. Squash should be tender-crisp, not mushy.

*STUFFED ZUCCHINI

Serve this as a side dish for barbecued, roasted, or broiled meats.

2 medium-sized zucchini	1 teaspoon minced parsley
1 small onion, chopped	¼ cup grated Parmesan cheese
1 small clove garlic, mashed	2 tablespoons fine bread crumbs
(or ½ clove)	dash of salt
1 teaspoon salad oil or olive oil	dash of pepper
1 egg, slightly beaten	

Wash zucchini and cut off ends. Cook whole in boiling salted water for 7 minutes or until tender but not mushy. Cool. Cut in half lengthwise and scoop out the seeds and center pulp, leaving thick shells. Reserve center pulp. Arrange halves with cut side up in a shallow baking pan or on an ovenproof serving dish.

Cook onion and garlic in oil; add the parsley, cheese, crumbs, zucchini pulp, salt, and pepper. Blend in the egg. Spoon stuffing into the shells. Bake in a moderately slow oven (325°) for 20 minutes or until lightly browned.

ZUCCHINI AU GRATIN

2 medium-sized zucchini	dash of salt and pepper
1 small onion, chopped	⅓ cup crushed cracker crumbs
1 tablespoon salad oil	½ cup shredded Cheddar
1 egg	cheese

Wash zucchini and cut off ends. Chop fine and blend with the onion. Heat oil in pan, and add squash and onion. Cook for 10 minutes, stirring over medium heat. Beat egg and blend with the vegetables. Cook until egg is set, about a minute. Season with salt and pepper. Turn mixture into two individual casserole dishes and top with cracker crumbs and cheese. Cover and bake in a moderate oven, 350°, for about 15 minutes or until cheese is melted.

To serve four: Double all quantities.

To serve six: Triple all quantities. You may wish to use a large casserole when serving this number of people. For 4 servings, a 1- or 1½-quart casserole is sufficient; for 6, a 2-quart casserole is needed.

POTATOES ANNA

1 pound small potatoes	1 teaspoon salt
3 tablespoons butter	chopped fresh parsley

Peel the potatoes and slice very thin—about ¹⁄₁₆ inch thick. (You should have about 4 cups of potato slices.) Butter generously an ovenproof bowl or a deep, straight-sided dish. Line the sides and bottom with potato slices to make a layer; sprinkle with salt and chopped fresh parsley, and continue layering until potatoes are used up. Pack them down well. Cover tightly with foil or with a buttered round of heavy paper. Bake in a hot oven (450°) for 45 minutes or until potatoes are tender when you insert a knife or skewer down the center. Unmound carefully onto a heated platter. There should be a crispy golden crust on the outside; the center should be tender, soft, and white flecked with green.

To serve four: Double the quantities and use a 2-quart casserole or bowl. Increase cooking time by 10 minutes; test with skewer to be sure.

To serve six: Triple the quantities and use a 3-quart casserole or bowl. Increase cooking time by 15 minutes.

*SPICED POTATOES

Remember these if you'd like to impress your mother-in-law. The potatoes are cut in wedge shape, sprinkled with seasoned salt, and broiled. They make a pretty garnish for a roast. But try them out for just two first.

2 medium-sized potatoes	melted butter
boiling salted water	seasoned salt

Cook the potatoes in their jackets in boiling water for about 15 minutes or until toothpick inserted into center of potato goes in easily but potato still has good shape. Drain and cool. Remove peeling. (These preliminaries can be done much ahead of time.) Cut potatoes in half lengthwise, and then cut each lengthwise half into quarters, making wedge shapes. Brush with butter and sprinkle with seasoned salt. Put on heatproof tray and slip under broiler, about 4 inches from heat. Broil for 5 minutes or until potatoes are tinged a golden color.

POTATOES RUDY

3 large baking potatoes	⅓ cup heavy cream
2 tablespoons butter	2 tablespoons grated Parmesan
½ teaspoon salt	cheese
freshly ground pepper	

Scrub the potatoes and cook in boiling water until tender, about 20 minutes. Cool, then peel them.

Heat the butter in a pan and brown the potatoes in it. Add the salt and pepper. Transfer potatoes into 2 buttered individual serving dishes or *au gratin* dishes. Pour the heavy cream on top and sprinkle with the Parmesan cheese. Slip under broiler until top is bubbly and browned and potatoes are hot all the way through.

To serve four: Double all quantities.

To serve six: Triple all quantities and put browned potatoes into a large casserole or *au gratin* dish if you wish.

*NEW POTATOES WITH HERBS

There's nothing quite like the *really* small new potatoes. Alas, they come but once a year. During the rest of the year, we must resort to just small potatoes.

8 to 10 hot cooked tiny new potatoes, scraped	½ cup sour cream
salt to taste	1 tablespoon *each* minced parsley and chives

Season the hot cooked potatoes with a sprinkling of salt. Combine the sour cream, parsley, and chives, and spoon the mixture over the potatoes. Serve immediately.

*FLAMED SWEET POTATOES

Just for fun, try this spectacle by the light of a candle!

8-ounce can whole sweet potatoes	brown sugar
salt	2 tablespoons warmed Jamaica rum or brandy

Slice the potatoes into a small casserole or a chafing dish. Sprinkle with salt and then with brown sugar. Heat, stirring carefully, until the brown sugar glazes the potatoes. Keep hot over a candle-warmer or in a chafing dish with very low flame. Add a dollop of butter, if you wish. At the table, pour the rum or brandy over, ignite, and shake pan until flames die. Serve.

*NEW POTATOES WITH LEMON

6 to 8 small new potatoes,   2 tablespoons butter
  scraped   ½ teaspoon grated lemon rind
boiling salted water   1 teaspoon chopped chives
             1 teaspoon lemon juice

Cook the new potatoes in salted water until tender. Drain. Meanwhile, combine the butter, lemon rind, chives, and lemon juice, and heat. Pour hot mixture over drained potatoes before serving, and toss lightly until each potato is well coated.

Salads and Salad Dressings

There can always be a salad! And a well-balanced meal *will* always have a salad or some other uncooked vegetable or fruit.

An old Spanish proverb says: "It takes four persons to make a salad—a spendthrift for the oil, a miser for the vinegar, a counselor for the salt, and a madman to stir them up."

A book published during the reign of Richard II (1390) called *The Forme of Cury* (the art of cookery) gives a recipe for a salad:

> Take parsley, sage, garlyc, young onyons,
> leek, borage, myntes, poireetes, fenel and
> cresses, rue rosemary and parslain lave and waithe
> hem clene; pick hem plucke hem smalle wyth
> thyne honde and myng hem wel wyth rawe oyl,
> lay on vinegar and salt and serve ye forth.

You have to let your imagination interpret for you. By any standard, this must have been a mighty heftily flavored salad!

Old cookery books go into great detail about the healthful aspects of salads—how they make the gastric juices flow and how good they are for digestion. They can also be both beautiful and delicious. Almost any vegetable or fruit is good in a salad if it is properly handled, so there is room for real creativity in the salad category.

In the Scandinavian countries they serve a salad on bread. Marinated cooked peas mixed with tiny bits of celery and onion, fresh

175

herbs, and a light creamy dressing may top thin slices of dark buttered bread. Sometimes this salad-sandwich is also topped with tiny cooked shrimp. What a great idea!

In California, the salads often are dinner-plate size. Many kinds of greens are available there, and it seems that the greater the variety, the greater the salad. One of my fondest memories is of a lovely salad bowl of greens topped with freshly ground pepper and a light oil-vinegar dressing added at the very last moment.

When you are cooking for two, try new combinations of greens and other fresh vegetables. Experiment with herbs and different flavored vinegars. See the difference a really fine olive oil makes. Try concocting your own dressings—many recipes are provided here for starters. But use any salad dressing sparingly—you want to enhance rather than hide the flavor of the greens.

After buying the salad greens, wash them well in cool water before storing them. (There's no need to use icy-cold water that numbs the fingers.) Dry the leaves well, and wrap loosely in paper toweling; then put them in the refrigerator.

Tear, rather than cut, the greens for a salad—the salad will look prettier, and the leaves will escape the bruising that makes them turn brown. However, I often do shred iceberg lettuce with a sharp knife just before serving.

By all means, do *not* put the dressing on until the very last possible minute. In fact, it can be added at the table. You can have everything else in the salad—herbs (try growing these and use them fresh), fruits, vegetables, sticks of cheese, or meat—but the dressing murders the poor lettuce leaf and makes it lose its juices and therefore its crispness.

Recipes that can be doubled or tripled without further instruction are marked with an asterisk (*).

*BASIC GREEN SALAD

2 to 3 cups crisp salad greens, washed
French Dressing (see Index)

salt and freshly ground pepper to taste

Use a combination of greens for interesting flavor.

Wash lettuce and dry well. Tear into bite-size pieces. A mixture of leaf lettuce, romaine, endive, and iceberg lettuce makes a flavorful salad, but you will have to go by what is in season unless you are lucky to have them all available most of the time. Rub the salad bowl with a cut clove of garlic. Add the lettuce, and pour on enough French Dressing to make the greens glossy. Toss well. Add salt and freshly ground pepper according to individual taste.

*GREEN GODDESS SALAD

Make Basic Green Salad, and add 1 cup cooked diced lobster, shrimp, crab, or chicken for each two servings. Dress with Green Goddess Salad Dressing (see Index) instead of French Dressing.

*GREEN SALAD PARMESAN

Make Basic Green Salad, and add ¼ cup grated Parmesan cheese (per each two servings) after French Dressing is added.

*LETTUCE AND TOMATO SALAD

Make Basic Green Salad, and add 2 peeled, diced tomatoes to the greens for each two servings.

*LETTUCE AND EGG SALAD

Make Basic Green Salad, and add 2 chopped hard-cooked eggs to the greens for each two servings.

*CHEF'S SALAD

Make Basic Green Salad, and add 1 small tomato, peeled and diced, 1 cup diced cooked chicken meat, 2 slices bacon cooked crisp and crumbled, 2 hard-cooked eggs (halved or quartered lengthwise), and ½ cup cheese (Cheddar or Swiss) cut in matchstick pieces, for each two servings. Dress with French Dressing, and toss lightly.

ICEBERG LETTUCE SALAD

¼ medium-sized head iceberg   ½ cup Vegetable, French, Blue
   lettuce   Cheese, or Combination
                                         Cheese Salad Dressing
                                         (see Index)

Cut lettuce into two wedges and stand on salad plates. Spoon dressing over and serve.

To serve four: Use ½ medium-sized head iceberg lettuce and ¾ to 1 cup dressing.

To serve six: Use ¾ head iceberg lettuce, cutting into wedges as directed above, and 1 cup to 1¼ cups of your favorite dressing.

AUTUMN SALAD

8-ounce can grapefruit   crisp lettuce
   segments, chilled   French Dressing (see Index)
1 small avocado, peeled and
   sliced

Arrange the grapefruit segments and avocado on crisp lettuce. Serve with French Dressing added to taste.

To serve four: Double the quantities, using a 16-ounce can of grapefruit segments.

To serve six: Triple all quantities.

*MANDARIN ORANGE–AVOCADO SALAD

Make Autumn Salad (preceding recipe), but use 1 cup drained, canned mandarin orange segments in place of the grapefruit segments. Make the same substitution when serving four or six.

*ORANGE AND GRAPEFRUIT SALAD

Make Autumn Salad, but use ½ cup each grapefruit segments and drained, canned mandarin orange segments in place of the entire amount of grapefruit. (Save remaining fruit, and serve chilled for breakfast a couple of days later.)

*CITRUS SALAD

1 tablespoon honey	⅛ teaspoon Angostura bitters
1 tablespoon white wine	dash of salt
vinegar	1 fresh grapefruit, peeled
½ teaspoon ground cardamom	1 large orange, peeled
crisp lettuce	

Combine the honey, vinegar, cardamom, bitters, and salt. Cut the grapefruit into segments and slice the orange. Arrange the fruit on lettuce-lined salad plates, and drizzle the dressing over.

*PINEAPPLE-APRICOT SALAD

You can always have a salad if you keep canned fruits on hand. If your supply of lettuce is low, then use it just to line the plate or as a garnish. Leftover canned fruits can be refrigerated for several days or frozen for later use. I prefer to remove fruits from the cans—even though it is perfectly safe to use the cans as storage containers—and avoid that "tinny" taste.

2 slices canned pineapple, drained	Sour Cream Dressing (see Index)
crisp salad greens	1 tablespoon minced walnuts
2 halves canned apricots, drained	

Arrange the pineapple slices over salad greens on individual serving plates. Top with canned apricot halves and a dollop of the Sour Cream Dressing. Sprinkle with walnuts.

*BANANA-PINEAPPLE SALAD

Canned sliced pineapple is a handy staple to keep in the cupboard, but even the smallest can has too many slices. Use what you need, and put the remainder in a plastic sandwich bag, with enough of the juice to keep it moist. Fasten with a twister and refrigerate or freeze until another day. This salad is especially good with pork or poultry.

1 medium-size banana
juice drained from pineapple
finely chopped nuts—about ¼ cup

2 slices canned pineapple
crisp salad greens
mayonnaise

Cut the banana in half crosswise and dip the halves in pineapple juice. Roll in chopped nuts. Arrange the pineapple slices on individual plates lined with salad greens. Top with the nutted bananas. Thin the mayonnaise with a bit of the pineapple juice, and serve in a bowl to spoon over the salad at the table.

*ICEBERG LETTUCE WITH HOT BACON DRESSING

2 wedges iceberg lettuce, about
   1 to 1½ inches thick
2 slices bacon, diced
1 teaspoon brown sugar
2 tablespoons sliced green
   onion

dash of salt
2 teaspoons vinegar
pinch of dry mustard
dash of paprika

Arrange the lettuce wedges on a serving platter. Cook the bacon in a small frying pan over low heat until crisp. Add the sugar, onion, salt, vinegar, mustard, and paprika. Bring to boiling point and remove from heat. Just before serving, pour the hot dressing evenly over the lettuce wedges, dividing the dressing equally.

*BACON, EGG, AND TOMATO SALAD

1 tomato, peeled

2 strips bacon, diced, cooked, and drained (reserve fat)

2 hard-cooked eggs, quartered

2 cups salad greens, cut in bite-size pieces

2 tablespoons hot bacon fat

French Dressing (see Index)

salt and pepper

To peel the tomato, dip in boiling water for 1 minute. Remove and slip off skin. Cut in quarters. Mix with bacon, eggs, and salad greens. Sprinkle the hot bacon fat and dressing over the salad, and toss lightly. Add salt and pepper to taste at the table.

CRANBERRY RASPBERRY SALAD

For holiday meals, this salad will add a spark of color as well as provide the cranberry that's so traditional.

½ cup thawed, frozen raspberries

1 package (1 tablespoon) unflavored gelatin

¼ cup of raspberry syrup (drained from the berries)

water

1 cup whole cranberry sauce (canned is fine)

1 tablespoon lemon juice

Drain the raspberries, reserving the syrup. Combine the gelatin with ¼ cup of the raspberry syrup to soften. Measure remaining syrup and add enough water to equal 1 cup of liquid. Heat to boiling. Stir into the softened gelatin until it is dissolved. Add the cranberry sauce, lemon juice, and raspberries. Turn into 2 individual-size (about ¾ cup each) salad molds. Chill until firm. Serve on a leaf of lettuce.

To serve four: Double the quantities.

To serve six: Triple the quantities, but you may wish to use a larger, 5- to 6-cup, salad mold.

HOT CHICKEN OR TURKEY SALAD

1 cup cooked chicken or turkey, cubed (can be leftover)
1 cup diced celery (about ¼-inch pieces)
¼ cup toasted slivered almonds
1 tablespoon chopped onion
¼ teaspoon salt
pinch of savory or chervil
1 tablespoon lemon juice
¼ cup *each* mayonnaise, sour cream, and shredded Cheddar cheese
paprika

In a mixing bowl combine the chicken, celery, almonds, onion, salt, savory, lemon juice, mayonnaise, and sour cream. Toss until well blended. Spoon into two individual baking dishes, scallop shells, or large custard cups. Sprinkle with the Cheddar cheese and paprika. Bake in a very hot oven (450°) for 10 minutes. Serve hot, garnished with a sprig of parsley.

To serve four: Double all quantities, and use 4 baking dishes or a 1-quart casserole.

To serve six: Triple all quantities, and use 6 individual baking dishes or a 1½-quart casserole.

*FRANKFURTER CUCUMBER SALAD

This is different, and also a good way to use any extra cooked frankfurters you have on hand.

4 cooked frankfurters, thinly sliced
1 cup diced peeled cucumber
1 cup cooked frozen peas
¼ cup French Dressing (see Index)
salad greens

Combine the frankfurters, cucumber, peas, and French Dressing, and chill. Serve on crisp salad greens.

*CRAB LOUIS

1 head iceberg lettuce
1 pound fresh crabmeat
2 tomatoes
2 hard-cooked eggs, peeled
½ cup mayonnaise
2 tablespoons heavy cream

2 tablespoons chili sauce
1 chopped green onion
2 tablespoons chopped green
  pepper
lemon wedges
salt and pepper to taste

On individual dishes, arrange large leaves of lettuce. Shred inner lettuce and mound over the leaves. Put crabmeat over the shredded lettuce. Cut the tomatoes and eggs into wedges, and arrange over the crabmeat. Chill.

To make the dressing, blend mayonnaise, cream, chili sauce, onion, and pepper. Pour over the salad. Serve garnished with lemon wedges, and add salt and pepper to taste at the table.

*SPICY OYSTER COCKTAIL SALAD

This makes two good-sized servings, and is very colorful. Try serving it in stemmed sherbet dishes or in scallop shells.

¼ cup tomato catsup
2 teaspoons lemon juice
1 teaspoon grated fresh
  horseradish
1 teaspoon Worcestershire
  sauce
1 teaspoon sugar
dash of Tabasco sauce

1 tablespoon minced mild
  onion
1 tablespoon minced celery
8-ounce can whole oysters,
  drained and quartered
crisp lettuce
1 small tomato, diced

In a small bowl, blend the catsup, lemon juice, horseradish, Worcestershire, sugar, Tabasco, onion, and celery. Arrange the oysters in two crisp lettuce cups. Pour sauce over all, and garnish with the diced tomato. Chill thoroughly before serving.

*MEAT AND POTATO SALAD

Use any leftover roast such as lean pork, lamb, beef, or chicken in this potato salad.

1 cup thinly sliced cold cooked meat
1 cup sliced cooked potato
⅓ cup French Dressing (see Index)

1 tablespoon minced green onion
salt and pepper to taste
salad greens

Combine the meat, potato, dressing, and green onion. Taste; then add salt and pepper. Serve chilled on crisp salad greens.

*AVOCADO SHRIMP BOAT

Salads make a fine luncheon dish—and this one is very good. It will especially please the avocado fans. The avocado is served in its "shell" for easier handling and serving, but peel it if you wish, and place the filled halves on a bed of lettuce instead.

1 large avocado
lemon juice
1 medium tomato, peeled and chopped
1 teaspoon sugar
¼ teaspoon salt
dash of black pepper
1 teaspoon chopped fresh parsley

1 green onion, minced
1 teaspoon vinegar
dash of cayenne
1 tablespoon French Dressing (see Index)
½ cup cooked tiny shrimp
crisp lettuce or watercress

Halve the avocado and remove the seed, being careful not to damage the avocado pulp. Rub pulp with lemon juice to prevent darkening. Combine the tomato with the sugar, salt, pepper, parsley, onion, vinegar, cayenne, French Dressing, and shrimp, tossing lightly. Pile this mixture into the cavities of the avocado shells. Garnish with lettuce or watercress, and serve immediately.

*TUNA-EGG SALAD

½ cup tuna, drained (half a   3 stalks celery, diced
   7-ounce can)   salt to taste
3 hard-cooked eggs, chopped   mayonnaise
                  salad greens

Combine the tuna (put remainder of can in a plastic bag, close, and freeze), eggs, celery, salt, and enough mayonnaise to hold the mixture together. Blend well, and chill. Serve on crisp salad greens.

*GREEN BEAN SALAD

1½ cups cooked green beans,   chopped chives
   chilled   1 finely chopped hard-cooked
½ cup celery, chopped   egg for garnish
French Dressing (see Index)

Combine the green beans, celery, and French Dressing. Cover and chill at least 30 minutes. Serve garnished with chopped chives and hard-cooked egg.

*ALMOND COLESLAW

2 cups finely shredded cabbage   ¼ cup toasted slivered almonds
¼ cup diced celery   ¼ cup mayonnaise
¼ cup diced cucumber   1 tablespoon cream
2 tablespoons minced green   1 tablespoon vinegar
  pepper   dash of seasoned salt
½ small onion, minced   paprika for garnish

Blend the cabbage, celery, cucumber, green pepper, and onion, and chill. Add the almonds just before serving. Blend the mayonnaise, cream, vinegar, and salt and mix into the vegetables. Sprinkle with paprika, and serve.

*SALADE NIÇOISE

crisp leaf lettuce
2 tomatoes, peeled and
  quartered
½ sweet onion, sliced
½ green pepper, sliced
2 radishes, trimmed and sliced
2 stalks celery, sliced

1 can (about 6 ounces) tuna,
  drained
4 anchovy fillets
1 hard-cooked egg, quartered
4 ripe olives, sliced
Salade Niçoise Dressing (see
  Index)

Wash lettuce, separating leaves, and dry them well. Divide between two salad bowls or serving plates, lining each completely. Top with the sliced tomatoes, onion, pepper, radishes, celery, and tuna (in chunks), dividing ingredients evenly between the two servings. Garnish with the anchovy fillets, hard-cooked egg, and sliced olives. Pour salad dressing on top (use entire amount), and serve. Add salt and freshly ground pepper to taste.

CELERY VICTOR

1 small heart of celery
1 small onion, peeled and
  sliced
1 beef bouillon cube
1 cup water
½ cup garlic French Dressing
  (see Index)

crisp lettuce
freshly ground pepper
anchovy fillets and pimiento
  strips
cherry tomatoes and ripe olives

Trim off root and leaf end of celery heart. Wash well to remove all grit. Put celery and onion in shallow pan; add bouillon cube dissolved in the water. Simmer 15 minutes or until they are tender. Remove from heat and cool in the liquid. Remove celery. Cut it in half lengthwise. Pour French Dressing over the halves and chill several hours. To serve, drain and arrange on crisp lettuce. Grind pepper over. Garnish with anchovy fillets, pimiento, tomatoes, and olives.

To serve four: Double all quantities.

To serve six: Triple all quantities. For either four or six, you may prefer to serve the Celery Victor on one large platter rather than in individual dishes.

*ITALIAN SALAD

1 cup chopped fresh parsley
½ cup cooked diced potatoes
2 hard-cooked eggs, chopped
1 cup cooked ham, cut in shoe-
string pieces

¼ cup Italian Dressing (see
Index)
crisp salad greens

Mix parsley, potato, eggs, and ham. Chill thoroughly. Blend in the dressing, and serve over crisp salad greens.

*SALADE DE MACARONI

A fine main-dish salad to serve in the summertime—especially good to tote along on a picnic.

⅓ cup macaroni
boiling salted water
½ cup ripe olives, chopped
½ cup canned tuna, drained
1 hard-cooked egg, diced

1 cup finely shredded cabbage
¼ cup mayonnaise
1 teaspoon prepared mustard
1 tablespoon vinegar
½ teaspoon salt

Cook the macaroni in boiling salted water until tender. Drain. Rinse well with cold water, and drain again. In a large bowl, combine the macaroni with the olives, tuna, egg, and cabbage. In a smaller bowl, combine the mayonnaise, mustard, vinegar, and salt. Lightly stir this dressing into the salad. Chill well before serving.

*ICEBERG LETTUCE AMANDINE

2 cups shredded iceberg lettuce   salt and pepper
3 tablespoons butter   1 tablespoon lemon juice or
2 tablespoons slivered almonds   vinegar
1 teaspoon sugar

Put the lettuce into a salad bowl and chill until serving time. Heat butter in pan and add the almonds; sauté for 1 minute or until almonds are lightly browned. Add the sugar. Add a dash each of salt and pepper, and the lemon juice or vinegar. Heat until bubbling. Pour over the lettuce, toss lightly, and serve immediately.

*TUNA SALAD IN PASTRY SHELLS

Serve this as a luncheon main dish or as a first course at dinner.

pastry or 1-crust pie (see Index)   1 can (about 6 ounces) tuna,
8-ounce can green beans,   drained and flaked
   drained, or 1 cup cooked   ½ cup mayonnaise
   fresh green beans, drained   salt and pepper to taste
8-ounce can kidney beans,   parsley for garnish
   drained

Divide pastry into two parts. Roll each out and fit each into an individual-size pie pan (about 4 inches in diameter). Prick all over with a fork. Chill. Bake shells in a very hot oven (425°) for 10 to 12 minutes, or until they are golden. Cool and remove from pans.

Combine the green beans, kidney beans, tuna, and mayonnaise. Add salt and pepper to taste. Chill well. Just before serving, fill the pie shells with the tuna mixture, and garnish with parsley.

Note: You can buy tiny tart shells already baked, and freshen them by heating for 5 minutes in a 350° oven.

*CHEDDAR CHEESE SALAD

Serve this salad as a main dish. With buttered toasted French bread or rolls and a fresh-fruit dessert, it makes a satisfying meal.

1 cup diced sharp Cheddar cheese
½ small onion, finely chopped
½ cup diced celery
2 hard-cooked eggs, finely chopped

2 tablespoons chopped fresh parsley
French Dressing or homemade Mayonnaise (see Index)
crisp lettuce

In a mixing bowl, combine the cheese, onion, celery, eggs, and parsley. Toss together lightly and chill. Add just enough dressing to moisten the salad and hold it together. Serve over crisp lettuce.

*HOT BACON AND LETTUCE SALAD

2 wedges of head lettuce
1 strip bacon, diced
1 tablespoon vinegar

1 tablespoon water
¼ teaspoon salt
dash of paprika

2 tablespoons sour cream

Arrange lettuce on a flat serving dish. Cook bacon until it is crisp; add the vinegar, water, salt, and paprika, and mix well. Pour over lettuce so that dressing filters between the leaves. Top each wedge with a tablespoon of sour cream.

*WILTED LETTUCE SALAD

Follow the directions in the preceding recipe for Hot Bacon and Lettuce Salad, but instead of iceberg lettuce, use 3 cups of leaf lettuce, washed, drained, and torn into bite-size pieces.

*HEARTS OF LETTUCE WITH CREAM DRESSING

Here's a salad to serve when cutting calories. Heavy cream has only half the calories of oil, and it adds the richness that is desirable in a salad dressing. Total count here is only about 125 calories.

1 very small head butter lettuce   1 tablespoon lemon juice
   (or Bibb or leaf lettuce)   1 tablespoon sugar
2 tablespoons heavy cream

Wash and thoroughly drain the lettuce, and break it into a salad bowl. Combine the cream, lemon juice, and sugar and pour over the lettuce, tossing gently. Serve immediately.

*WALDORF SALAD GOURMET

Here's a salad that makes an especially good flavor combination with barbecued poultry or spareribs. The salad dressing and the apple-celery mixtures can be assembled in advance, to save time just before dinner. If the apples are diced more than a half-hour in advance, sprinkle them with a bit of lemon juice to prevent their turning brown.

¼ cup commercial sour cream   1 tablespoon white wine
1 teaspoon sugar   vinegar
¼ teaspoon salt   1 cup diced unpared apple
dash of pepper   ¼ cup finely diced celery
pinch of tarragon   crisp lettuce leaves
              2 tablespoons minced pecans

Blend the sour cream, sugar, salt, pepper, tarragon and vinegar. Chill. Just before serving, blend this mixture with the apple and celery. Turn out onto lettuce-lined salad plates. Top each serving with the nuts.

*ASPARAGUS SALAD

½ package (10-ounce size) frozen asparagus pieces
½ head romaine lettuce
1 tablespoon diced pimiento
1 green onion, chopped
2 tablespoons toasted sesame seed
⅛ teaspoon freshly ground pepper
⅛ teaspoon crumbled tarragon or basil
1 tablespoon fresh lemon juice
1 tablespoon salad oil
salt to taste

Cook the half-package of asparagus according to directions on the box. (Wrap remaining asparagus tightly and return to freezer.) Drain and chill the cooked asparagus. Break lettuce into bite-size pieces and put into a chilled salad bowl. Add asparagus, pimiento, green onion, and sesame seed. Mix the pepper, tarragon, lemon juice, and salad oil. Just before serving, pour the dressing over the greens, and toss well. Add salt to taste.

CAULIFLOWER TOSSED SALAD

1 cup sliced raw cauliflower
2 tablespoons French Dressing
½ small avocado
2 tablespoons sliced, stuffed green olives
1 tomato, peeled and diced
2 to 3 tablespoons crumbled Roquefort or blue cheese
crisp greens

Cover cauliflower with ice water and chill for 1 hour; drain well. Pour French Dressing over and let stand for 2 hours. Just before serving, toss with the avocado, olives, tomato, and cheese. Serve on crisp greens.

To serve four: Double the quantities, using half of a medium-sized head of cauliflower.

To serve six: Triple the quantities, and use a whole head of cauliflower.

*BELGIAN ENDIVE SALAD

Belgian endive is a very special, usually imported, salad green. You can recognize it by the slender pale heads about 4 to 6 or 7 inches in length, with tapering ends. This dressing is especially good with Belgian endive, but it should be made in advance (even the night before) so the flavors have time to blend.

1½ teaspoons salad oil
1 teaspoon lemon juice
½ teaspoon prepared hot
    mustard
dash of cinnamon
¼ teaspoon curry powder

dash of salt
2 tablespoons chopped filberts,
    walnuts, or pecans
2 small heads Belgian endive,
    split lengthwise

Combine the oil, lemon juice, mustard, cinnamon, curry powder, salt, and nuts, and let stand at least one hour for flavors to blend. Just before serving, split the endive, and spoon the dressing over. This is just the right amount for 2 salads.

CAESAR SALAD

3 tablespoons olive oil or salad
    oil
½ cup toasted croutons
1 small clove garlic, mashed, or
    ½ large clove
½ head romaine or other
    crisp lettuce

dash of salt
freshly ground pepper
2 tablespoons lightly beaten
    egg
juice of ½ lemon
2 anchovy fillets, chopped
2 tablespoons Parmesan cheese

Combine oil, croutons, and garlic. Let stand several hours. Rub salad bowl with a cut clove of garlic. Tear lettuce into bite-size pieces and put into the bowl. Sprinkle with salt and grind on a generous amount of pepper. Just before serving, pour oil and crouton mix on top. Toss lightly until lettuce is glossy. Add the egg and lemon juice, and toss again. Add anchovies and Parmesan cheese, and serve immediately.

To serve four: Double all quantities, but instead of the beaten egg, boil 1 egg 1 minute (*just* 1 minute!); cool it and break it into the salad.

To serve six: Triple all quantities, but follow same instructions for egg as given for four servings.

*MIXED VEGETABLE SALAD

It's handy and economical to buy the frozen mixed vegetables in a bag—you can scoop out just what you need for two servings.

1 cup frozen mixed vegetables	dash of salt
boiling salted water	½ teaspoon dried dillweed (or
2 teaspoons chopped parsley	chopped fresh dill)
1 small green onion, chopped	¼ teaspoon sugar
1 teaspoon vinegar	¼ cup mayonnaise

crisp salad greens

Cook the vegetables in boiling salted water 2 minutes less than directed on the package, so that they remain a bit firm. Remove from heat, drain, and chill. Blend in all the remaining ingredients except the salad greens. Chill at least a half-hour; then heap onto plates lined with the salad greens.

*MEDITERRANEAN SALAD

½ small head iceberg lettuce	2 tablespoons orange juice
¼ cup pitted, sliced ripe olives	1 tablespoon vinegar
1 peeled orange, sliced	½ teaspoon salt
2 tablespoons salad oil	¼ teaspoon paprika

Break lettuce into bite-size pieces. Arrange in salad bowl; add the olives and orange slices. Blend the oil, orange juice, vinegar, salt, and paprika together well. Just before serving, pour dressing over the salad and toss lightly.

*COMBINATION SALAD WITH BROWNED BUTTER

lettuce to line salad plates	1 large avocado, peeled, sliced
1 large tomato	2 green onions, cut in ½-inch
salt and pepper to taste	pieces
2 tablespoons butter	

Arrange the lettuce leaves on two salad plates. Slice the tomato, and arrange the slices on the lettuce leaves. Sprinkle lightly with salt and pepper. Arrange the sliced avocado over the tomato. Top with green onions. Heat butter until it is lightly browned (not burned), and pour over the salads. Serve immediately.

*LIMELIGHT MUSHROOM SALAD

The flavor combination of fresh mushrooms and lime juice is delicate and very pleasing. Make this salad ahead, though, for the flavors are best if the mushrooms and seasonings chill at least one hour.

¼ pound fresh mushrooms, thinly sliced	juice of 1 lime
3 tablespoons olive oil	freshly ground pepper
2 tablespoons chopped chives	salt
¼ teaspoon crushed tarragon leaves	crisp lettuce

Put the sliced mushrooms into a bowl. Combine oil, chives, tarragon, lime juice, and a good sprinkling of pepper, and pour the mixture over the mushrooms. Cover and chill (you can do this in the morning and let it chill all day). Toss mushrooms and dressing together, add salt to taste, and serve over crisp lettuce leaves.

*GERMAN POTATO SALAD

Serve this salad German style with a good-quality Bratwurst for supper.

3 medium-sized potatoes	⅓ cup bouillon
4 slices bacon, diced	1 teaspoon salt
1 small onion, diced	¼ teaspoon pepper
⅓ cup vinegar	1 teaspoon sugar
	1 egg yolk, beaten

Scrub the potatoes and boil them in their jackets; cool and peel. Cut in ¼-inch slices. Cook bacon until crisp; add the onion, and stir and cook until it is transparent. Add the vinegar, bouillon, salt, pepper, and sugar. Stir and bring to a boil. Add the egg yolk, stirring vigorously. Remove from heat and pour over the potatoes.

ZUCCHINI SALADE FRANÇOISE

½ pound (small) zucchini	1 small clove garlic, cut
1 cup water	1 cup chopped head lettuce
¼ teaspoon salt	2 green onions, chopped
	French Dressing (see Index)

Slice zucchini into ¼-inch pieces. Cook in boiling water with salt added, for 3 minutes. Drain and chill. Rub salad bowl with the cut clove of garlic. Combine chilled zucchini, lettuce, and onions in bowl and dress with the French Dressing, tossing until ingredients are glossy. Serve immediately.

To make four servings: Double all ingredients except garlic; you need only 1 clove of garlic for the bowl.

To make six servings: Triple all ingredients. Again you will need just 1 clove of garlic.

*FRESH BEEFSTEAK TOMATO SALAD

1 large beefsteak tomato,   2 teaspoons olive oil
   thickly sliced   ⅛ teaspoon fresh basil, or dried
lettuce   basil soaked in 1 teaspoon
salt   water to freshen
freshly ground pepper

    Arrange tomato slices on crisp lettuce. Sprinkle with salt and grind pepper over them. Spoon olive oil over them, and sprinkle with basil. Refrigerate until serving time.

SCANDINAVIAN TOMATO SALAD

    For a colorful salad that you can arrange on plates ahead of time, try this one.

½ cup commercial sour cream   crisp salad greens
1 tablespoon white wine   2 medium-sized tomatoes,
   vinegar   thinly sliced
3 tablespoons salad oil   ¼ cucumber, peeled and sliced
¼ teaspoon salt   salt and pepper
1 tablespoon dillweed   dillweed or parsley for garnish

    In a small bowl combine the sour cream, vinegar, salad oil, salt, and dillweed, and chill. Serve this dressing in a bowl at the table.
    Line two salad plates with the crisp greens. Arrange the tomatoes and cucumber over the greens. Sprinkle lightly with salt and dillweed or parsley. Spoon dressing on at the table.

To serve four: Double all quantities.

To serve six: Triple the quantities of the salad itself, but just double the quantity of dressing as the serving for two or four is very generous.

*AVOCADO-TOMATO SALAD

1 large tomato, peeled	⅛ teaspoon salt
1 large avocado, mashed (about	½ teaspoon tarragon leaves
¾ cup)	¼ cup sour cream
1 tablespoon lemon juice	crisp lettuce

Cut tomato into 4 slices. Blend avocado with lemon juice, salt, tarragon, and sour cream. For each serving, lay a tomato slice on crisp lettuce, and top with some of the dressing. Add the second tomato slice, and frost each serving with the remaining dressing.

*QUICK TOMATO SALAD

When time is short and you've chosen to grill chops or steaks, this salad is a snap to prepare—especially for anyone foresighted enough to keep a few good homemade salad dressings ready in the refrigerator.

2 tomatoes cut in wedges	½ cup of any homemade salad
crisp greens	dressing (see Index)

Arrange tomatoes on crisp greens, and top with dressing. (When serving four or six, you may prefer to arrange the salad on a platter instead of individual plates, and offer a selection of salad dressings.)

*COOKED VEGETABLE SALAD

1 cup cooked mixed vegetables,	salt and pepper
chilled (such as carrots, peas,	½ cup Vegetable or French
lima beans, green beans,	Dressing (see Index)
chopped broccoli)	crisp greens
1 cup diced cooked potato	

Toss the cooked vegetables together, taste, and season with salt and pepper and French Dressing. Arrange over crisp greens. Serve as a main-dish salad with hot rolls and dessert.

*SWISS SALAD

½ cup diced Swiss cheese
½ cup cooked green beans
½ cup finely diced celery
½ small head of lettuce broken
   into bite-size pieces

½ cup parsley, coarsely
   chopped (remove stems)
French Dressing (see Index)

Toss all ingredients together except dressing. Turn into chilled salad bowl. Just before serving, add the French Dressing until the salad ingredients are nicely coated and shiny. Toss lightly, and serve.

*FRUIT AND VEGETABLE SALAD

11-ounce can mandarin orange
   sections
1 medium-sized apple, cored
   and diced (not peeled)

½ cup finely shredded raw
   carrot
1 cup finely diced iceberg
   lettuce

Oriental Poppy Seed Dressing
to taste (see Index)

Drain the oranges and combine them with the apple, carrot, and lettuce. Chill. Toss lightly. Add dressing to moisten sufficiently.

*TOMATO AND DILL PICKLE SALAD

2 medium-sized tomatoes,
   peeled
lemon juice
2 teaspoons chopped fresh dill
   or dillweed

2 teaspoons chopped capers or
   dill pickle
½ teaspoon olive oil or salad oil
freshly ground pepper
salt to taste

Slice the tomatoes and arrange on a platter. Sprinkle with lemon juice and a mixture of the dill, capers or pickle, and oil. Sprinkle with pepper and chill well. Add salt to taste at the table.

CRISP SPINACH SALAD

fresh spinach, about ¼ pound
3 tablespoons olive oil or salad
   oil
1 tablespoon white wine
   vinegar

1 tablespoon chopped fresh
   parsley
salt and pepper
2 slices bacon, cooked crisp and
   crumbled

Wash the spinach leaves very well, and dry them. Tear into bite-size pieces. (Do this early in the day and store them in a plastic bag in the refrigerator.) Just before serving, put spinach into a salad bowl. Sprinkle oil on top, using more or less to taste. Then add the vinegar, parsley, salt, and pepper; toss lightly but well. Divide between individual salad bowls, and sprinkle with the crisp bacon to garnish.

To serve four: Double the amounts, but go easy on the vinegar— add the same amount of vinegar as for two; then slowly add more, tasting to be sure the salad is not too sour.

To serve six: Triple the amount of spinach and bacon. Double remaining ingredients, and season to taste with salt and pepper.

*MINTED POTATO SALAD

2 cups cooked potatoes, diced
   and chilled
⅓ cup French Dressing (see
   Index)

1½ teaspoons chopped mint
   leaves, fresh or dried
1 green onion, minced
salt and pepper to taste
   salad greens

Combine the potatoes, French Dressing, mint, and onion. Taste; then add salt and pepper. Cover and chill. Serve over a bed of crisp salad greens.

*LEAF LETTUCE WITH LEMON AND CREAM

If you have a garden lettuce, here's a way to serve it.

2 to 3 cups well-washed young   1 tablespoon lemon juice
  lettuce leaves   salt and pepper to taste
2 tablespoons heavy cream   dash of sugar

Wash and dry the lettuce, and break into small bite-size
pieces; chill until serving time. Pour cream over and toss lightly.
Sprinkle with the lemon juice, salt and pepper, and sugar, and
toss again. Serve immediately.

*NUTTED COLESLAW

2 cups finely shredded cabbage   ¼ cup walnuts or pecans,
¼ cup diced celery   chopped
¼ cup diced cucumber   ¼ cup mayonnaise
2 tablespoons minced green   1 tablespoon cream
  pepper   1 tablespoon vinegar
2 green onions, minced   ¼ teaspoon salt
                          paprika

Combine cabbage, celery, cucumber, green pepper, and onion,
and chill. Just before serving, add the walnuts. Blend together
the mayonnaise, cream, vinegar, and salt. Pour over vegetables,
and mix lightly. Sprinkle top with paprika for color.

*MANDARIN CARROT SALAD

¾ cup shredded raw carrots   ¼ cup mayonnaise
¼ cup seedless raisins   salt to taste
1 tablespoon lemon juice   salad greens
11-ounce can mandarin
  oranges, drained

Combine the carrots, raisins, lemon juice, and oranges, and chill. Just before serving, blend in the mayonnaise and salt. Serve on a bed of crisp salad greens.

*FRESH MUSHROOM SALAD

¼ pound small white mushrooms, washed
1 tablespoon fresh lemon juice
2 tablespoons olive oil
1 teaspoon *each* finely chopped chives and fresh parsley

crisp leaf lettuce, washed
salt and freshly ground pepper to taste

Slice the mushrooms and put into a bowl. Add the lemon juice, olive oil, chives, and parsley. Toss lightly. Chill for 2 hours before serving (to allow flavors to blend). To serve, line salad bowls with lettuce and arrange mushrooms over; sprinkle with additional fresh parsley. Add salt and freshly ground pepper to taste.

HEARTS OF LETTUCE WITH FRENCH DRESSING

Prepare butter, Bibb, or leaf lettuce as directed in the preceding recipe for Hearts of Lettuce with Cream Dressing, using a very small head of lettuce for two servings. Just before serving, add French Dressing (homemade—see Index; or commercial) according to taste.

To serve four: Use a single large head of lettuce.

To serve six: Use 2 medium-size heads—or about 2 quarts of greens.

*SPINACH SALAD WITH HOT BACON DRESSING

This is a favorite of mine, especially when I can get the tiny fresh spinach leaves in the summertime.

½ pound fresh spinach, washed well, dried, chilled
2 slices bacon, diced
1 teaspoon brown sugar
2 tablespoons sliced green onion

dash of salt
2 teaspoons vinegar
pinch of dry mustard
dash of paprika

Snip the spinach with scissors coarsely into a salad bowl. (Be sure you've washed out *all* sand!) Cook the bacon in a small frying pan over low heat until it is crisp. To it, add the sugar, onion, salt, vinegar, mustard, and paprika. Bring to boiling point and remove from heat. Just before serving, pour the hot dressing over the spinach and toss lightly until leaves are coated.

SALAD DRESSINGS

FRENCH DRESSING

¼ cup lemon juice or white wine vinegar
¾ cup salad oil
1 teaspoon salt

¼ teaspoon pepper
½ teaspoon paprika
½ teaspoon sugar
¼ teaspoon dry mustard

Shake all ingredients together in a jar until they are blended. Store in refrigerator until ready to use. Dressing will separate, but shake again just before serving. Makes about 1 cup of dressing.

GARLIC FRENCH DRESSING

Make French Dressing and add 1 clove of garlic, minced or mashed.

FRENCH DRESSING FOR FRUIT SALAD

1 cup salad oil	¼ cup pineapple juice or juice
4 tablespoons lemon juice	from canned pineapple
½ cup fresh orange juice	1 teaspoon salt
2 teaspoons sugar or to taste	

Put all ingredients into a jar. Cover tightly and shake until blended. Store dressing in refrigerator. Makes 2 cups.

HONEY FRENCH DRESSING

½ cup *each* salad oil and honey	1 teaspoon salt
½ cup white wine vinegar or	½ teaspoon celery seed
cider vinegar	

Put all ingredients into a jar, cover tightly, and shake them until they are well blended. Dressing separates on standing; shake again just before serving. Store in refrigerator. Makes 1½ cups.

*SALADE NIÇOISE DRESSING

1 tablespoon lemon juice	3 tablespoons olive oil
1 teaspoon basil	

Mix ingredients well and serve with Salade Niçoise, a tossed green salad, or over sliced tomatoes. This quantity is enough for salads for two. For four servings, double the recipe; for six, triple it.

COMBINATION SALAD DRESSING, SWISS STYLE

¼ pound blue cheese   ½ teaspoon tarragon
8-ounce cream cheese   ½ teaspoon salt
¼ cup grated sapsago cheese   dash of pepper
    (Swiss import)   1 small clove garlic, mashed
          ½ cup (or more) light cream

Blend the blue cheese, cream cheese, and sapsago together.
Add the tarragon, salt, pepper, and garlic. Slowly blend in the
cream, beating with mixer until dressing is smooth and thick. For
the right consistency for a dressing, it may be necessary to add
slightly more cream (or milk). Makes about 2½ cups of dressing.

COMBINATION CHEESE DRESSING, AMERICAN STYLE

Prepare the same as the preceding recipe, but omit the sapsago
cheese. Makes about 2 cups.

VEGETABLE SALAD DRESSING

1 onion, chopped fine   1 cup salad oil
4-ounce can chopped pimientos   ¾ to 1 cup sugar (to taste)
1 green pepper, seeded and   1 tablespoon salt
    chopped   ¾ cup vinegar

Put onion, pimiento, and green pepper into the blender, and
purée. (Or use a food chopper with a fine blade.) Blend in the
oil, sugar, salt, and vinegar until all ingredients are well mixed.
Store in refrigerator. Makes about 1 quart of dressing.

THOUSAND ISLAND DRESSING

1 cup mayonnaise   2 tablespoons chopped stuffed
½ cup sweet pickle relish,   olives
    drained   2 green onions, chopped

Blend all ingredients together and store in refrigerator. Makes about 1¾ cups of dressing.

GREEN GODDESS SALAD DRESSING

10 anchovy fillets, chopped fine
2 green onions, chopped fine
4 tablespoons minced parsley
1 tablespoon (more or less) crumbled tarragon leaves

4 tablespoons minced chives
¼ cup tarragon wine vinegar
3 cups mayonnaise (preferably homemade)

Mix together the anchovies, onions, parsley, tarragon, chives, and vinegar. Let stand 5 minutes. Blend in the mayonnaise. Store extra dressing in the refrigerator; it keeps very well. Makes 4 cups of dressing.

ITALIAN DRESSING

4 slices bacon, diced and cooked crisp
¼ cup hot bacon drippings (the amount from 4 strips of bacon)
¼ cup oil

1 egg, beaten
¼ teaspoon dry mustard
¼ teaspoon black pepper
½ teaspoon salt
¼ cup white wine vinegar or lemon juice

1 tablespoon sugar

Cook the bacon in a heavy saucepan instead of frying pan. Add the oil to the hot drippings. Remove from heat, and cool them. Stir in the egg, seasonings, vinegar or lemon juice, and sugar, blending until smooth. Pour dressing over the chilled greens or refrigerate for use at a later time. After refrigerating, heat dressing slightly to melt bacon fat and homogenize the dressing. Makes 1 cup.

PINK ROQUEFORT DRESSING

1 cup *each* salad oil, catsup, and   1 clove garlic, mashed
   vinegar   4 ounces Roquefort cheese
1 medium-sized onion, finely   salt and pepper to taste
   chopped

Combine the salad oil, catsup, and vinegar until blended. Add the onion and garlic. Blend in Roquefort cheese, and mix well. Taste, then add salt and pepper. Store in refrigerator until ready to use. This dressing should stand a few hours before serving so that flavors will blend. Makes about 3 cups of dressing.

CREAMY ROQUEFORT DRESSING

½ cup crumbled Roquefort   ½ cup heavy cream
   cheese   ½ cup mayonnaise or sour
3-ounce package cream cheese,   cream
   softened   2 tablespoons fresh lemon juice
                   salt to taste

Mash the Roquefort and cream cheese together. Blend in the cream and mayonnaise or sour cream. Add the lemon juice. Store dressing in refrigerator. Makes about 1¼ cups.

SEAFOOD SALAD DRESSING

½ cup *each* mayonnaise and   1 tablespoon minced green
   sour cream   onion
¼ cup French Dressing,   ½ teaspoon crushed dried
   (commercial or homemade)   tarragon
1 small clove garlic, crushed   1 tablespoon chopped
   (optional)   anchovies

Mix the mayonnaise, sour cream, French Dressing, garlic, green onion, tarragon, and anchovies. Chill. Serve over crisp mixed greens, sliced onions, cooked and chilled shrimp, lobster, crab, or diced cooked chicken. Makes 1¼ cups.

SOUR CREAM SALAD DRESSING

This dressing is fine over coleslaw or on a wedge of iceberg lettuce. It keeps well in the refrigerator and is handy to have on hand as a "homemade" dressing for quick meals.

1 egg	½ teaspoon dry mustard
1 cup commercial sour cream	2 teaspoons sugar
¼ cup white wine vinegar	½ teaspoon dillweed
1 teaspoon salt	pepper to taste

Beat egg slightly in a bowl set over simmering water or in the top of a double boiler. Mix in the sour cream, vinegar, salt, mustard, sugar, dillweed, and pepper. Stir and cook over hot water until the dressing is smooth and thick. Cool. Makes 1¼ cups of dressing.

ORIENTAL POPPY SEED DRESSING

This dressing is ideal on sliced oranges arranged on crisp greens, or with a fresh fruit salad. Keep remaining dressing refrigerated.

⅓ cup honey	¾ cup salad oil
1 teaspoon salt	1 tablespoon finely chopped
2 tablespoons wine vinegar	onion
1 tablespoon prepared mustard	1 tablespoon poppy seeds

Combine honey, salt, vinegar, and mustard; gradually add the salad oil, beating until mixture is well blended. Add the onion and poppy seed (for a fruit salad you may prefer to omit the onion). Cover and chill several hours before serving, to allow flavors to blend. Makes about 1 cup dressing.

Vegetable and Meat Sauces

Sauces can be overdone, or they can truly embellish your cooking. A sauce as simple as melted butter and lemon juice will enhance the flavor of fish or asparagus—or even of mashed potatoes. A simple sauce with just a pinch of a herb or a squeeze of lemon can also dress up leftover foods.

This chapter is not intended to be a complete survey of all possible sauces. It presents those that we have enjoyed and some that are supporting items to certain other dishes in this collection.

There are on the market now many powdered sauces packed in sealed envelopes. These are a boon to the person who is not quite sure of a recipe, or needs the added support of the printed directions on the package. I seldom use them because I find that my own sauces made from scratch are much better tasting and less expensive, too.

Most sauce recipes make a definite quantity, and in cooking for two you do not always need the entire amount. Store leftover sauces in the refrigerator, covered.

BASIC WHITE SAUCE

2 tablespoons butter (1 for thin sauce, 2½ for medium, 4 for thick)
1 cup milk

2 tablespoons flour (1 for thin sauce, 2½ for medium, 4 for thick)
¼ teaspoon salt

Melt butter in a small saucepan. Add flour and stir until mixture is smooth. Slowly beat in the milk to make a lumpless, creamy mixture. Add salt. Heat slowly over low heat, stirring until sauce is thickened and smooth. Makes 1 cup sauce.

For Cream Sauce:
Make Basic White Sauce, using cream in place of milk.

Cheese Sauce:
Make Basic White Sauce. Add 1 cup shredded Cheddar cheese. Stir over low heat until cheese melts.

Curry Cream Sauce:
Make Basic White Sauce. Stir in 1 teaspoon (or more, according to taste) of curry powder.

QUICK HOLLANDAISE SAUCE

Make Basic White Sauce. Just before serving, stir in 2 egg yolks. Beat in 6 tablespoons soft butter, a bit at a time, and add 1 tablespoon lemon juice.

PARSLEY SAUCE

Make Basic White Sauce, and add ¼ cup chopped fresh parsley before serving.

MORNAY SAUCE

2 tablespoons butter	dash of pepper
2 tablespoons flour	1 cup shredded Gruyère, jack,
1 cup milk	or Cheddar cheese
½ teaspoon salt	

Melt butter in pan and stir in the flour. Remove from heat. Add milk, stirring mixture until it is well blended. Return to heat and cook until it is thickened. Add the salt, pepper, and cheese, and mix until cheese is melted into the sauce. (Makes about 2 cups.)

HOT TARTAR SAUCE (*for Fish*)

½ cup Basic White Sauce (see   1 teaspoon lemon juice or wine
   Index)   vinegar
½ cup mayonnaise   1 tablespoon sweet pickle relish
1 teaspoon finely chopped
   onion

Heat White Sauce and slowly beat in the mayonnaise. Add
onion, vinegar, and relish, and keep hot but don't boil. Serve immediately. Makes 1 cup sauce.

BÉCHAMEL SAUCE

2 tablespoons butter   ½ cup chicken broth
2 tablespoons flour   ½ cup light cream
                   salt to taste

Melt butter in pan and add flour, stirring until flour is just
lightly browned. Gradually add the chicken broth and cream, stirring constantly, and cook mixture until it is smooth and thick.
Taste. Then add salt. Makes 1 cup sauce.

CHEESE SAUCE

2 tablespoons butter   1 cup shredded sharp Cheddar
4 teaspoons cornstarch   cheese
2 cups milk   ¼ teaspoon paprika

Melt butter in pan and stir in the cornstarch and milk.
Cook, stirring constantly, until mixture is thickened. Add the
cheese and paprika and stir until mixture is smooth. For a richer
sauce, use cream in place of milk. Makes about 3 cups.

GRIBICHE SAUCE

3 hard-cooked eggs
4 teaspoons salad herbs
1 tablespoon hot mustard

1 cup salad oil
1 teaspoon vinegar
salt and pepper to taste

Separate yolks from whites. Mash yolks until smooth, and rub in the herbs and mustard. Beat in the oil slowly, keeping mixture very smooth. (Or use blender to mash yolks, add remaining ingredients, and slowly add the oil, keeping the blender on low speed all the while.) Blend in the vinegar and salt and pepper to taste. Last of all, add chopped egg whites. Serve cold. Makes about 1½ cups.

Note: This sauce can be refrigerated if left over. We do not recommend doubling the quantities. If you need a double quantity, make the recipe twice.

HORSERADISH–SOUR CREAM SAUCE

This is excellent served with rare roast beef, with Fondue Bourguignonne, or simply spooned over a grilled hamburger.

1 cup commercial sour cream
2 tablespoons grated fresh
  horseradish

¼ teaspoon salt
1 teaspoon lemon juice

Combine sour cream, horseradish, salt, and lemon juice. Let stand for about a half-hour before serving so that flavors can mellow. Makes about 1 cup sauce.

HOLLANDAISE SAUCE (*Blender Method*)

½ teaspoon dry mustard
½ teaspoon salt
3 egg yolks

1½ tablespoons fresh lemon
juice
1 tablespoon hot water

¾ cup hot melted butter

Combine mustard, salt, egg yolks, lemon juice, and hot water in blender container; process mixture at low speed a few seconds or until it is blended. Cover container and turn speed to "high." Remove cover and slowly pour in the melted butter in a steady, even stream. Sauce will thicken in about 30 seconds. If for some reason it does not, add a lump of softened butter—about 3 tablespoons or so. Makes about 1 cup sauce.

MOUSSELINE SAUCE

1 cup Blender Hollandaise
Sauce (see Index)

1 cup cream, whipped

Make Hollandaise Sauce (Blender Method) and keep it warm. Whip the cream, and fold it into the Hollandaise thoroughly. Add more salt and lemon juice if necessary. Makes 2 cups sauce.

TARTAR SAUCE

1 cup mayonnaise
3 tablespoons minced sweet
pickles
1 tablespoon white wine
vinegar

1 teaspoon chopped parsley
½ teaspoon Worcestershire
sauce
dash of salt and cayenne pepper

Blend all ingredients together well. Cover and refrigerate before serving, to allow flavors to blend. Makes about 1 cup.

MAYONNAISE (*Blender Method*)

2 tablespoons fresh lemon
  juice or white vinegar
½ teaspoon salt

½ teaspoon dry mustard
  or 1 teaspoon prepared
1 whole egg

1 cup salad oil

Combine lemon juice or vinegar, salt, mustard, and egg in the blender. Process at high speed a couple of seconds. Pour in about 2 tablespoons of the salad oil and process again at high speed; remove cover while blender is running and add the remaining salad oil in a slow, steady stream. Whirl until thick—about 2 minutes. Makes about 1½ cups.

HOT MAYONNAISE

Blend ¾ cup mayonnaise (commercial or made by preceding recipe) with 1 cup dairy sour cream, 2 tablespoons chili sauce, 1 chopped green onion, ½ minced green pepper, 2 tablespoons minced pimiento, 1 tablespoon wine vinegar, a dash of Tabasco, and 4 tablespoons white wine. Taste; then add salt if needed. Makes about 2 cups.

VINAIGRETTE SAUCE

Serve this one as a dipping sauce for Fondue Bourguignonne or hot fried shrimp or scallops.

3 tablespoons salad oil
1½ tablespoons white wine
  vinegar
¼ teaspoon salt

½ small clove garlic
1 teaspoon *each* minced pickle,
  parsley, green pepper, and
  chopped chives

Combine all ingredients, and blend them well. Refrigerate them until they are thoroughly chilled. Before serving, remove the garlic. Makes about ¼ cup sauce.

RÉMOULADE SAUCE

Try this on any cooked fish or shellfish. It is especially good as a dressing for seafood salad served as an appetizer course.

1 cup mayonnaise
2 green onions, finely minced
2 anchovy fillets, finely minced

1 teaspoon chopped capers
1 tablespoon chopped sour
   pickle

1 tablespoon minced parsley

Blend all ingredients together well, and chill. Makes about 1½ cups.

WHITE BUTTER SAUCE (*for salmon*)

Scandinavians serve a sauce like this over poached lutefisk at Christmastime. Try it.

1 green onion, finely chopped
1 tablespoon white wine
   vinegar

¼ cup soft butter
dash of pepper

Cook the onion and vinegar together until onion is golden. With a whip, beat in the butter in small bits until mixture is frothy and white.

CURRY SAUCE

Try this sauce on cooked lamb, veal, chicken, or seafood. It's a wonderful way to transform leftovers into a delicacy.

1 cup finely chopped onion
1 cup finely chopped tart apple
¼ cup shortening
1 clove garlic, crushed
2 tablespoons curry powder, or
   more to taste

¼ cup tomato catsup
2 cups beef or chicken stock
2 tablespoons fresh lemon
   juice
salt to taste

Cook the onion and apple in the shortening until soft. Add the garlic, curry powder, catsup, stock, and lemon juice. Taste; then add salt. Makes about 4 cups.

SAUCE VERTE

This sauce is excellent on all types of meats, such as meatballs, baked or poached chicken, and sliced cooked veal, pork, or turkey.

½ medium-sized head of lettuce, chopped	1 tablespoon melted butter ½ cup heavy cream

Cook the lettuce in the butter in a large frying pan until wilted. Then press it through a sieve or whirl it in a blender until it is smooth. Add the cream and simmer for 5 minutes. Add salt and pepper to taste. Makes about 2 cups of sauce.

BÉARNAISE SAUCE

A blender is a great help in making both Béarnaise and Hollandaise. You can use a whip or mixer, but it is messier.

3 egg yolks	1 tablespoon hot water
1½ tablespoons tarragon vinegar	½ teaspoon salt dash of cayenne
2 tablespoons chopped parsley	½ teaspoon dry mustard

¾ cup melted butter

Put egg yolks, vinegar, and parsley into blender container. Turn to low speed until ingredients are blended. Add the hot water, salt, cayenne, and dry mustard. With blender at high speed (put cover on or it will splash!), slowly pour in the melted butter in a steady stream. Process until thickened and smooth. Makes about 1 cup.

SWEET AND SOUR SAUCE

Serve this over leftover chunks of roast pork or chicken or on fried fish.

½ cup *each* vinegar and sugar
1 cup water
1 tablespoon cornstarch

1 cup crushed pineapple
1 teaspoon soy sauce
½ cup catsup

Combine vinegar, sugar, water, and cornstarch, and cook until mixture is thickened and smooth. Blend in the pineapple, soy sauce, and catsup. Makes about 3½ cups. This sauce can be stored, covered, in the refrigerator for about a week, or frozen and stored for up to 3 months.

DEVILED BUTTER

Serve this with cracked crab, hot lobster, or as a sauce for Fondue Bourguignonne.

1 cup melted butter
2 teaspoons prepared mustard
2 teaspoons Worcestershire
    sauce
3 dashes of Tabasco

2 tablespoons tomato catsup
2 tablespoons lemon juice
2 tablespoons chopped fresh
    parsley

Blend butter with mustard, Worcestershire, Tabasco, catsup, lemon juice, and parsley. Serve in dish with a candle-warmer underneath, to keep sauce hot. Makes about 1½ cups.

LEMON BUTTER

1 cup melted butter
dash of Tabasco
4 tablespoons fresh lemon juice

2 tablespoons chopped fresh
    parsley

Blend butter with the Tabasco, lemon juice, and parsley, and heat until mixture is bubbly. Serve in a dish with a candle-warmer underneath. Excellent with fish, shellfish, or roasted poultry. Makes about 1 cup sauce.

LEMON CREAM SAUCE

Marvelous on broiled fish or poached chicken breasts!

3 tablespoons butter	2 tablespoons lemon juice
½ cup whipping cream (do not whip)	salt and pepper to taste

Heat butter in top of double boiler. Add cream and lemon juice. Heat over simmering water, stirring. Taste, and correct seasonings. If desired, add a tablespoon of chopped herbs—a mixture of basil, tarragon, marjoram, and thyme. Makes ½ cup sauce.

TOMATO SAUCE

This sauce goes well over poached eggs, butter-sautéed fish, or sliced leftover roast beef.

2 medium-sized tomatoes	2 tablespoons chopped parsley
2 slices bacon, chopped	salt and pepper to taste
1 medium-sized onion, finely chopped	

Dip tomatoes in boiling water and slip off the skins. Cut tomatoes in half crosswise. Squeeze out the seeds. Chop tomato pulp and put into a pan. Cook over low heat until a thick purée is formed.

In another pan, cook the bacon until crisp. Add onion, and cook until it is soft. Add the tomato purée, parsley, and salt and pepper to taste. Press the mixture through a wire strainer or whirl it in a blender until smooth. Serve hot. Makes about 1 cup.

TARRAGON SAUCE

Excellent on cooked sliced turkey, veal, or beef. Try it also when serving Fondue Bourguignonne.

1 cup commercial sour cream
½ teaspoon crushed tarragon
2 tablespoons white wine
   vinegar (preferably with
   tarragon)

1 teaspoon seasoned salt
1 tablespoon chopped green
   onion
½ teaspoon sugar

Combine all ingredients well and let sauce mellow for about a half-hour before serving. Makes about 1 cup sauce.

ALL-PURPOSE BARBECUE SAUCE

Here's an old favorite all-purpose barbecue sauce. Use it for ribs, pork chops, or chicken. It is especially good on beef ribs, if you give them a thick glazing of it while they are on the grill.

1 cup brown sugar
8-ounce bottle catsup
1 tablespoon dry mustard
2 tablespoons Worcestershire
   sauce

3 tablespoons vinegar
1 teaspoon liquid smoke
   flavoring (optional)
1 cup strong coffee
1 onion, chopped fine

salt and pepper to taste

Combine all ingredients in a saucepan. Mix well and cook over medium heat, stirring occasionally. Simmer for a half-hour in all. Store the cooled sauce in a covered jar in the refrigerator, for use as needed. Makes about 4 cups.

FRUITED BARBECUE SAUCE

In place of the coffee, use 1 cup orange juice in the recipe for All-Purpose Barbecue Sauce. This variation is especially good on chicken.

GARLIC BARBECUE SAUCE

Follow the directions for All-Purpose Barbecue Sauce, and add 2 cloves garlic, crushed, to the sauce. This is good on beef and tender cuts of game suitable for barbecue.

AIOLI SAUCE

4 cloves garlic, mashed	2 egg yolks
½ teaspoon salt	1 cup olive oil
⅛ teaspoon pepper	2 teaspoons lemon juice

In a small bowl mix garlic, salt, and pepper; blend in the egg yolks. With a whip, slowly beat in the olive oil, beating constantly. Add lemon juice. If sauce curdles, add a few drops of lukewarm water, and whip vigorously.

This sauce can be made in a blender: First, put the garlic, salt, and pepper in the blender. Add eggs, and run at low speed a few seconds. With blender still at low speed, slowly add the oil, and continue to blend to make a smooth and thick sauce. Makes about 1¼ cups.

HOT ANCHOVY SAUCE

This sauce is great as a dip for fresh vegetables—an interesting appetizer! Serve it also as a dip for the beef chunks when serving a beef fondue. You can save what is left over in a covered jar in the refrigerator; it will be good for a couple of weeks. To serve, put the sauce in a dish over a candle-warmer, and keep it hot.

½ cup butter	1 tablespoon minced or
¼ cup olive oil	puréed anchovies
2 large cloves garlic, mashed	

Heat the butter, olive oil, garlic, and anchovies together in a pan, stirring until anchovies are evenly blended in the sauce. Serve hot as a dip.

MUSHROOM SAUCE

1 cup sliced fresh mushrooms   1 cup chicken stock
1 tablespoon butter   salt and pepper
1 tablespoon flour   ½ cup heavy cream
                    lemon juice

Sauté the mushrooms in butter for 5 minutes. Stir in the flour and chicken stock. Simmer 10 minutes. Season to taste with salt and pepper. Add the cream and lemon juice to taste. Serve over Russian Chicken cutlets. Serve immediately. Makes about 2 cups.

Desserts and Dessert Sauces

A dessert is the crowning touch to a meal, but it should be selected with care so that it does not overbalance the rest of the meal. An American tradition typifies exactly how *not* to select a dessert—the mince and pumpkin pies of Thanksgiving. This holiday meal is heavy enough already, and we add more "lead" at the end. But who am I to knock an established tradition? I serve mince and pumpkin pies at Thanksgiving, too!

In meal planning, take into account the "weight" of the entire meal. If there is much rich food, the dessert should be light. And vice versa. When in doubt, you can serve just fruit and cheese. But don't *always* skip dessert entirely—something a bit sweet and refreshing at the end of a meal is a delight to look forward to.

Recipes that can be doubled or tripled without further instruction are marked with an asterisk (*).

*FRUIT PLATTER

A fruit platter is prettiest with fresh strawberries, melons, apricots, and cherries. Select the fruit carefully. Clean and wash it well and arrange it on a platter. Cover and chill until ready to serve. Serve with whipped cream, flavored with a drop of mint extract, if you wish.

*CRÈME BRÛLÉE

⅔ cup whipping cream   1 tablespoon rum or ¼
2 egg yolks   teaspoon rum flavoring
2 tablespoons sugar   2 tablespoons finely chopped
dash of salt   toasted almonds
1 teaspoon vanilla   ¼ cup brown sugar

Heat cream to scald; *don't* boil. Beat egg yolks, sugar, and salt until they are blended. Stir the hot cream into the egg-yolk mixture. Set pan over simmering (not boiling) water, and cook and stir until mixture just coats the spoon. Remove from heat and place over cold water to cool. Add the vanilla, rum, and toasted almonds. Pour into two individual-size heatproof dishes, such as *au gratin* dishes, and chill, uncovered, for 4 hours. At serving time, sift the brown sugar over the tops to make an even layer, being sure to cover the entire surface. Preheat broiler. Set dishes in a pan of cold water. Broil about 3 inches from heat until sugar caramelizes—this takes just a few seconds. Serve immediately—with sliced fresh strawberries, if you wish.

*POTS DE CRÈME VANILLE

This classic French dessert is supposed to be made in the special little pots with covers; however, custard cups work very well even if they are not as glamorous.

2 egg yolks   1 tablespoon sugar
dash of salt   ¼ teaspoon vanilla
                      ⅔ cup heavy cream

Beat the egg yolks until they are light and thick. Add the salt, sugar, and vanilla. Stir in the heavy cream a little at a time, and divide the mixture between the tiny *pots de crème* or 4-ounce custard cups. Cover pots. (If using custard cups, cover each with foil.) Set in a pan of water and bake in a 350° oven for 35 minutes or until a knife inserted in the center comes out clean. Chill before serving.

CLASSIC DESSERT SOUFFLÉ

1½ tablespoons *each* butter
  and flour
⅓ cup light cream
dash of salt
2 eggs, separated
¼ cup sugar

grated peel of ½ orange
2 tablespoons orange-flavored
  liqueur, such as curaçao or
  triple sec
whipped cream flavored with
  a bit of liqueur

Melt butter in a pan and blend in the flour. Add cream and salt, and stir until mixture is smooth. Cook until it is thickened. Remove from heat, and beat in the egg yolks, 2 tablespoons of the sugar, the orange peel, and liqueur.

Whip whites of eggs until they hold soft peaks; then beat in remaining sugar until whites hold firm peaks. Fold the whites into the sauce. Pour into a buttered 1-quart soufflé dish. Bake in a moderately hot oven (375°) for 45 minutes. Serve with the flavored whipped cream.

To serve four: Double the quantities and bake in 1½-quart dish.

To serve six: Triple the quantities and bake in a 2-quart dish.

GRAND MARNIER SOUFFLÉ

Flavor Classic Dessert Soufflé with Grand Marnier liqueur in place of the orange flavor.

KAHLÚA SOUFFLÉ

Omit the orange peel and flavor the Classic Dessert Soufflé with Kahlúa.

CHOCOLATE SOUFFLÉ

2 tablespoons butter	1 tablespoon cocoa
½ cup sugar	2 eggs
1 tablespoon flour	1 teaspoon vanilla
⅓ cup milk	dash of salt

Butter the bottom and sides of a 3- to 4-cup soufflé dish or baking dish, using 1 tablespoon of the butter. Coat bottom and sides with 1 tablespoon of the sugar.

Melt the remaining butter and blend in the flour. Add milk gradually and cook, stirring, until thick and smooth. Stir in the cocoa and 2 tablespoons of the sugar. Separate the eggs and beat yolks until thick. Add a little of the hot mixture to the yolks, and then combine the two mixtures. Cook about 1 minute over low heat, stirring constantly, until it is thickened. Add vanilla.

Beat egg whites with salt until foamy; add remaining sugar and continue beating until stiff peaks form. Fold the chocolate sauce into the beaten whites. Turn into the prepared soufflé dish or casserole dish, and bake in a hot oven (400°) for 25 minutes. Serve immediately.

To serve four: Double the quantities and bake for 30 minutes.

To serve six: Triple the quantities; bake for 35 minutes or until soufflé feels set on top when touched lightly—but the center must still be creamy or the soufflé will taste dry.

*ORANGE MARMALADE SOUFFLÉ

2 egg whites	⅓ cup chopped toasted
pinch of salt	almonds
2 tablespoons sugar	1 egg yolk
2 tablespoons orange	dash of salt
marmalade	¼ cup sugar
butter	½ cup whipping cream

Beat egg whites with salt until they are stiff; gradually add the sugar and orange marmalade. Butter the top of a double boiler generously. Sprinkle with the almonds. Carefully pour in the egg-white mixture. Cover and steam for 1 hour. Just before serving, beat egg yolk with salt and sugar until blended. Whip the cream until it is stiff, and fold it into the yolk. Flavor with a liqueur such as Cointreau, if you wish. Turn soufflé out onto a serving dish and pour sauce over the top.

SALZBURGER NOCKERLS

A classic dessert that is surprisingly simple to do. It comes out with a delicate, rich flavor, and is not too high in calories either.

2 eggs, separated	2 tablespoons butter
4 tablespoons sugar	Vanilla Sugar (see below)
1 tablespoon flour	shaved chocolate

Beat the egg whites until they are foamy; then add the sugar and beat until they are stiff. Beat the egg yolks with the flour until they are thick and light. Carefully fold the egg-white mixture into the egg-yolk mixture.

Over low heat, melt butter in a frying pan or an ovenproof metal tray until butter bubbles and just begins to brown. With heat still at low, spoon egg mixture into the pan in two large mounds. Cook for 1 minute. Place in a moderately slow oven (325°), and bake for 7 minutes or until tops are slightly golden. Sprinkle with Vanilla Sugar, and serve immediately. Sprinkle with shaved chocolate at the table.

To serve four: Double the quantities and shape into 4 mounds before baking.

To serve six: Triple the quantities and shape into 6 mounds before baking.

VANILLA SUGAR

Sift 1 cup powdered sugar, and put it into a jar with tight-fitting lid. Put 2 inches of a vanilla bean into the jar and store for 24 hours before using (remove vanilla bean before using). Or store 1 cup granulated sugar in the same way. Both powdered and granulated sugar are excellent bases for Vanilla Sugar, and go well with the Salzburger Nockerls.

*MEXICAN CHOCOLATE PUDDING

1 square (1 ounce) unsweetened chocolate	¼ teaspoon cinnamon dash of salt
½ cup milk	½ teaspoon vanilla
¼ cup sugar	1 egg
¼ cup whipping cream	

Shave the chocolate into the top of a double boiler. Mix with milk, sugar, cinnamon, and salt. Heat over hot water until chocolate is melted. Beat with rotary beater until mixture is smooth. Add vanilla and unbeaten egg; beat 1 minute. Cover and cook for 40 minutes. Do *not* lift cover during this time. Serve warm with sweetened whipped cream.

*QUICK CUSTARD CREAM

This is a dessert that can be eaten like a custard—with a spoon; or it can be used as a sauce over fruit. It is to be served warm. For convenience, have all ingredients already measured into a bowl before you sit down to eat. Then take just a few minutes to whip up the dessert before serving.

2 egg yolks	2 tablespoons sugar
2 teaspoons curaçao, kirsch, or any favorite liqueur	

Mix the yolks, liqueur, and sugar in a small bowl. Set it over a pan of simmering water, and with a rotary beater or whip, beat until it is thick and hot. Do *not* let water boil or the mixture will curdle. Pour into sherbet dishes or wineglasses (or use as a sauce over fresh berries or fruit), and serve immediately.

*STRAWBERRIES WITH QUICK CUSTARD CREAM

Quick Custard Cream (see Index)

1½ cups sliced fresh strawberries

2 teaspoons sugar

Make the Custard Cream first. Divide strawberries into serving dishes, and sprinkle with sugar. Divide the cream between the servings. Chill well.

*PEACH HONEY TARTS

1 cup sliced fresh peaches
2 tablespoons honey
¼ cup sour cream
¼ cup whipping cream, whipped

2 prepared tart shells (pastry; you can buy them)

Put the sliced peaches into a bowl. Blend 1 tablespoon of the honey with the sour cream, and mix this into the peaches gently. Blend remaining tablespoon of honey into the whipped cream, and put about a tablespoon of this mixture into each of the tart shells. Divide the peach mixture between the 2 shells, and top with remaining whipped cream. Chill it 2 hours before serving.

*POT DE POMMES or *"Apple Pot"*

Another French classic. This one is not unlike our apple crisp, but I think the French name sounds more elegant.

2 large firm tart cooking   2 tablespoons butter
  apples, peeled, cored, sliced   ¼ cup sugar
  thin   2 tablespoons flour
¼ cup sugar mixed with   dash of cinnamon
  1 teaspoon cinnamon   dash of salt
                ¼ cup butter

Use two individual *pot de pomme* pots or one ovenproof dish that holds about 3 cups. Put a layer of apples in the bottom of the dish. Sprinkle with cinnamon sugar and dot with butter. Repeat layering until apples are then used up. In a bowl, blend the second ¼ cup sugar, the flour, cinnamon, salt, and butter until the mixture resembles fine crumbs. Sprinkle over the apples. Bake in a moderate oven (350°) for 45 minutes or until apples are tender. Serve hot or cold with a bowl of cream whipped with a pinch of salt and a dash of lemon juice and sweetened with brown sugar. Sprinkle servings with black walnuts, if you have them.

GINGERED PLUMS

8-ounce can greengage plums or   1 slice candied ginger, chopped
  purple plums   heavy cream

Mix plums with ginger in two individual dessert dishes, and refrigerate them until serving time. Serve with heavy cream, letting each person add cream to his own preference.

To serve four: Use the 1-pound can of plums; double the ginger.

To serve six: Use 3 (8-ounce) cans of plums, and triple the amount of ginger.

*BANANAS FLAMBÉ

2 bananas, green tipped
2 tablespoons butter
2 tablespoons brown sugar

3 tablespoons warm Cointreau
or rum
heavy cream

Peel the bananas and cut in half both lengthwise and cross-wise. Melt butter in chafing dish over direct flame or in flat frying pan over high heat. Add the bananas, cut side up. Cook them quickly until they are browned; turn them over, sprinkle with the sugar, and cook until sugar has dissolved. Add the Cointreau or rum, ignite, and shake pan until flames die. Serve with sauce from pan and cream to pour over each serving.

*STRAWBERRIES WITH SOUR CREAM

A simple and elegant way to serve fresh strawberries when they are in season.

1½ cups sliced fresh
strawberries
¼ cup light brown sugar

½ cup commercial sour cream
brown sugar for topping

Put strawberries in a dessert bowl, and sprinkle with the ¼ cup brown sugar. Top with the sour cream, and sprinkle with a small additional amount of brown sugar. Chill at least an hour.

*MELON WITH PORT

1 small cantaloupe
2 tablespoons sugar

¾ cup port, Marsala, or red
wine

Cut cantaloupe in half. Remove seeds and scrape clean. Sprinkle each half with sugar, and put 6 tablespoons of port into the center of each. Chill at least 1 hour. Serve as a first course or as dessert.

BUTTERED PINEAPPLE SPEARS

¼ medium-sized fresh   ¼ cup butter
  pineapple

Cut top and peel off pineapple. Cut fruit in half lengthwise and remove the tough core. Slice ¼ of the pineapple into ½-inch spears. (Wrap remaining pineapple in plastic, and refrigerate.) Heat butter in frying pan and brown the spears quickly, over high heat, being careful not to burn them. Serve with pancakes or waffles for breakfast.

To serve four: Use ½ of the pineapple and ½ cup butter.

To serve six: Use the whole pineapple and ¾ cup butter.

*BAKED STUFFED APPLES

Bake apples for dessert when you already have the oven going anyway. You can easily double or triple the batch, and have some left for dessert another night. They're good chilled and served with cream to be poured over them, and a dash of nutmeg.

2 large tart baking apples   ⅓ cup *each* chopped dates or
                                     raisins, chopped nuts, water,
                                     sugar, and currant jelly

Core the apples and peel halfway down. Mix the dates (or raisins) with the chopped nuts. Fill the apple cavities with the mixture. Put apples into two buttered 8-ounce custard cups. Combine the water, sugar, and jelly, and pour over the apples, dividing it evenly between the two. Sprinkle the apples with additional granulated sugar and bake in a moderate oven (350°) for about 45 minutes or until they are tender but not mushy. Baste occasionally with the juices. (To bake 4 or more apples, use an 8- or 9-inch square pan.)

*PEARS CARDINAL

Keep the makings for this dessert on hand. It is a quick one to do.

8-ounce can pear halves
½ cup strawberries fresh or
   frozen, thawed

2 tablespoons sugar
slivered toasted almonds
sweetened whipped cream

Chill the pear halves; drain well. Put the strawberries through a wire sieve or whirl them in a blender until puréed. Sweeten with the sugar. Arrange pear halves, cut side down, in two dessert dishes. Spoon the strawberry mixture over and sprinkle with the almonds. Serve with whipped cream.

*WINTER DESSERT

1 orange, peeled and sliced
1 apple, cored and sliced
1 banana, sliced

3 to 4 tablespoons powdered
   sugar
3 to 4 tablespoons sweet sherry
   or Marsala

Layer the orange, apple, and banana in two dessert dishes, sprinkling each layer with some of the sugar. Pour the sherry or Marsala over all, and chill thoroughly before serving.

When making desserts for more than two, you may prefer to use a glass dessert bowl rather than individual dishes.

*FRUIT AND CHEESE

Fruit and cheese almost always complement a meal. Fresh pears sliced and served with thin wedges of provolone, fresh grapes or apricots served with cream cheese, and crisp apples served with a sharp Cheddar are popular combinations.

*ORANGE-BROILED BANANAS WITH ICE CREAM

1 banana, peeled
1 tablespoon butter, melted
¼ cup brown sugar, firmly
  packed
¼ cup orange juice

1 teaspoon grated orange peel
1 teaspoon chopped candied
  ginger
1 cup (2 scoops) vanilla ice
  cream

Cut the banana in half lengthwise and crosswise, to make 4 pieces. Arrange pieces in a baking dish in a single layer. Pour melted butter over. Mix the sugar, orange juice, orange peel, and candied ginger, and pour over the bananas. Broil, 8 inches from source of heat, for 5 minutes or until bananas are glazed. Serve hot, topped with a scoop of ice cream. Spoon some of the sauce over the ice cream.

CHANTILLY FIGS

Especially for those who are lucky enough to have fresh figs!

6 fine ripe figs
1 cup *each* sugar and water

whipped cream flavored with
vanilla

Wash and dry the figs. Combine sugar and water in a saucepan, and simmer 5 minutes. Add the figs, and cook for 4 to 5 minutes. Cool them in the syrup. Drain them, and reserve syrup. Serve the figs chilled, with whipped cream.

To serve four: Double the quantity of figs but not of the syrup.

To serve six: Triple the quantity of figs but not of the syrup; use the same amount as given above.

Note: The sugar-water syrup can be kept for use another time. It's an excellent liquid for poaching other fresh fruits too, such as pears, apples, etc.

*GREEN GRAPES WITH SOUR CREAM

1 cup green grapes, halved   2 tablespoons maple sugar or
                                       brown sugar
                      sour cream

Arrange the green grapes in two dessert dishes well ahead of
time. Sprinkle them with the sugar (you can be more lavish with
sugar if you wish). Cover liberally with sour cream. Chill at least
2 hours before serving.

*BANANAS AU RHUM

1 tablespoon butter   1 teaspoon lemon juice
2 large bananas, sliced   1 tablespoon water
2 tablespoons brown sugar   2 tablespoons rum
                      heavy cream

Heat butter in frying pan. Add bananas, sugar, lemon juice,
water, and rum. Cook over moderate heat for 5 minutes, stirring
occasionally. Serve with cream.

*STRAWBERRIES FLAMBÉ

1½ cups halved strawberries   2 tablespoons cognac or brandy
3 tablespoons sugar   heavy cream

Put strawberries into a heatproof pan or chafing dish before
you begin the meal. Sprinkle them with sugar. Set over a candle-
warmer or over lowest heat on the range. The berries should heat
very slowly while you are eating the main part of the meal. To
serve, put the cognac or brandy into a small metal dish or large
spoon. (A metal ¼-cup measure with a long handle is fine.) Heat
cognac over a candle or low heat until it is just warm. Ignite it,
then pour it over the strawberries. Spoon strawberries into dessert
dishes, and serve cream at the table.

*FRENCH FRUIT CROÛTES

If you have on hand any such fruits as peaches, apricots, or bananas that are getting too ripe—and if you also happen to have leftover cake that is getting a bit dry—this dessert is just for you.

2 slices dry cake (any flavor), sliced ½ inch thick	sliced fresh peaches, apricots, or bananas
2 tablespoons butter	whipped cream, slightly
2 tablespoons berry or fruit jam	sweetened
dash of nutmeg	

Spread the cake slices on both sides with the butter, and heat slices in frying pan until both sides are golden. Spread each slice with jam, and arrange slices on serving plates. Place the fruit on top of the jam spread, heap on whipped cream (or sour cream), and top with a dash of nutmeg.

*FLAMBÉED PEACHES

2 fresh peaches, sliced	¼ cup kirsch, Cointreau, triple
2 tablespoon butter	sec, or curaçao
2 tablespoons sugar	

Heat the peaches and butter in a frying plan over medium-high heat, turning them gently until peaches are coated with melted butter. Add the sugar and two tablespoons of the liqueur. Pour into serving dishes. Heat remaining liqueur until it is just warm. Touch it with a lighted match, pour it over the fruit, and serve immediately—with cream, if you wish.

Note: This dessert can also be made with canned sliced peaches. For 2 servings, use an 8-ounce can of sliced peaches; for 4 servings, use a 16-ounce can.

DESSERT SAUCES

Using dessert sauces is a quick way to produce a grand finale for a meal. These are some of my favorites.

*CHANTILLY SAUCE

Serve this sauce over fresh berries or fruit, ice cream, or cupcakes, or put it in cream-puff shells or individual tart shells.

½ cup cream, whipped
2 tablespoons powdered sugar
2 tablespoons fruit pulp
(mashed pulp of the fruit over which you will serve the

sauce) *or* 1 tablespoon Cointreau or fruit-flavored liqueur, *or* 1 teaspoon vanilla

Whip the cream, adding powdered sugar and flavoring. Serve over fresh fruit or ice cream, or follow any of the suggestions given above. Makes about 1 cup sauce.

QUICK MELBA SAUCE

¼ cup raspberry jelly or jam

1 cup raspberries, fresh or frozen, thawed

Heat the jelly or jam until it is liquid. (Strain, if using raspberry jam, to remove seeds.) Press raspberries through strainer; blend with the heated mixture. Chill and serve over poached or canned peach halves filled with a scoop of ice cream. Makes about ¾ cup.

HOT MELBA SAUCE

Follow directions for Quick Melba Sauce, but heat sauce to simmering and serve hot over fruit or ice cream.

SCANDINAVIAN DESSERT BUTTER SAUCE

2 egg yolks	1 tablespoon grated fresh
⅓ cup sugar	lemon rind
⅓ cup melted butter	2 tablespoons lemon juice

½ cup cream, whipped

Beat egg yolks until they are thick, and gradually add the sugar. Blend in the melted butter, lemon rind, and juice, mixing until it's smooth. Fold in the whipped cream. Serve over hot puddings or cake or fresh berries. Makes about 1½ cups sauce.

SWEDISH VANILLA SAUCE

Serve this one over hot baked apple turnovers. (Try the refrigerated dough type, which are quite good and quick to make.) Or serve over homemade apple dumplings, steamed puddings, or angel food cake and berries.

1 cup sugar	4 tablespoons butter
1 cup boiling water	1 teaspoon vanilla
1 tablespoon cornstarch mixed with 2 tablespoons water	

Blend sugar and water. Add the cornstarch, mixed to make a smooth paste, to the sugar-water mixture, and cook it until thickened. Stir in the butter and vanilla. Serve hot. Makes about 2 cups of sauce.

SWEDISH BROWN SUGAR VANILLA SAUCE

Make Swedish Vanilla Sauce, but use brown sugar in place of the granulated sugar. Serve over gingerbread or hot chocolate-cake squares.

HARD SAUCE

Serve this classic over steamed puddings (either homemade or bought), or over hot gingerbread or chocolate cake.

¼ cup soft butter
1 cup sifted powdered sugar
⅛ teaspoon salt

1 teaspoon vanilla or a fruit-flavored liqueur

Cream the butter and sugar until they are blended. Add the salt and flavoring, and whip until very fluffy. Serve in small bowl to spoon over individual servings of a hot pudding or cake. Makes about 1½ cups.

DANISH BROWN SUGAR SAUCE

½ cup butter
1 cup packed brown sugar
1 egg

1 tablespoon white vinegar
dash of nutmeg
1 teaspoon vanilla

1 cup heavy cream, whipped

Melt butter in pan over very low heat and blend in the brown sugar and egg, along with the vinegar and nutmeg. Using a hand beater, whip while mixture is warming until it is very light and fluffy; continue whipping for 10 minutes, or until sauce is thickened. Add the vanilla. Fold in the whipped cream. Excellent over steamed puddings, sliced bananas, poached pears, or pound cake. Makes 2½ cups of sauce.

Breads and Basic Pastry

A crusty bread is always welcome at the table. In cooking for just two, here's where the freezer can come in handy. Instead of baking bread in the conventional-size pan, try to find small pans, 3¼ by 5½ inches. A recipe that yields one loaf of bread (5- by 9-inch size) will yield three of the smaller-size loaves. Freeze two, and eat one fresh from each batch you make.

When thawing frozen bread, put it into the oven while it is still frozen—it will come out as fresh-tasting as if it were just baked. Bread is more successfully frozen after, rather than before, baking. Cool the loaves on a rack first. Then wrap them well in plastic bags, foil, or plastic wrap, and seal tightly. Thaw at room temperature, wrapped, or unwrap and place in a preheated oven. Normally, the oven should be set at about 350°; a small loaf will thaw in the oven in about ten minutes. However, if you're already baking something, pop the bread into the oven along with the other food regardless of the oven temperature—bread isn't fussy!

The frozen and refrigerated doughs on the market today make it quite simple to serve freshly baked bread. For those who like to do it from "scratch," here are carefully selected recipes.

BASIC YEAST BREAD

¼ cup lukewarm water
1 package yeast, dry or
 compressed
2 cups lukewarm milk

2 tablespoons melted butter or
 shortening
2 tablespoons sugar
1½ teaspoons salt

6 to 6½ cups all-purpose flour

Pour water into bowl and add yeast, stirring until it is dissolved. Add the milk, butter, sugar, and salt. Add half the flour and beat well—until batter is very smooth and all flour lumps are gone. Slowly beat in all the remaining flour except the last ½ cup. Sprinkle this ½ cup of flour onto a board or clean counter top, and turn dough out onto it. Cover with a bowl for 15 minutes to allow dough to "rest."

Then knead dough by folding the mass over onto itself, rotating the mass with each fold. (*Note:* Do not poke your fingers into the dough; rather, work by cupping your hands around the dough and folding with the palms of your hands.) Knead until dough is very smooth and satiny—or until all flour appears to be worked thoroughly into it. Lightly grease the mixing bowl and put dough into it. Turn dough over once to grease the top of it.

Cover bowl and let dough rise in a warm place until it is doubled. Punch down. Cover and let rise again until it is doubled. Then divide dough into two parts (or into six parts if using small pans), and make a smooth ball of each part. Place each in a bread pan. Let it rise until it is doubled again.

Bake in a 375° oven for 35 to 45 minutes, or until loaves sound hollow when tapped. Brush tops with butter if desired, and turn out onto a rack to cool. Cool before slicing. Makes 2 large loaves (5 by 9 inches) or 6 small loaves (3¼ by 5½ inches).

WHOLE WHEAT BREAD

Make Basic Yeast Bread exactly as directed, but use wholewheat flour instead of white flour.

MOLASSES RYE BREAD

Make Basic Yeast Bread exactly as directed, but substitute molasses for the sugar and replace half the flour with rye flour. (Rye-bread dough may be stickier than white-bread dough, so dust hands with flour when handling it.)

GRAHAM BREAD

Make Basic Yeast Bread exactly as directed, but use 3 cups of graham flour in place of 3 cups of the white flour. Use 2 tablespoons of light molasses instead of the sugar.

ONION BREAD

Make Basic Yeast Bread exactly as directed, but replace the milk with a 10½-ounce can of onion soup and enough water to equal 2 cups. Omit the salt and add 1 teaspoon instant onion instead.

*CURRIED BREAD SLICES

2 slices, 1 inch thick, French bread	2 tablespoons soft butter curry powder

Spread the bread with the butter, sprinkle with curry powder, and bake in a hot oven (400°) or slip under broiler (about 4 inches from the heat) until bread is lightly browned.

CARAWAY BUTTERED BREAD

Make as directed in the preceding recipe, but sprinkle bread slices lightly with caraway seeds.

SESAME BUTTERED BREAD

Make as directed under Curried Bread Slices, but sprinkle slices with sesame seeds before broiling.

HERBED BREAD

2 tablespoons softened butter   dash of garlic powder
1 tablespoon Parmesan cheese   ½ loaf brown-and-serve French
1 teaspoon chopped parsley   bread (wrap other half and
¼ teaspoon oregano   freeze)

Combine butter, Parmesan, parsley, oregano, and garlic powder. Slice the bread and spread with the herb butter. Lay on a cookie sheet and bake in a hot oven (400°) for 10 minutes.

HERBED ENGLISH MUFFINS

For each serving use the following amounts:

1 English muffin   1 teaspoon dried herbs (chives,
2 teaspoons butter   oregano, basil, parsley)
            2 tablespoons chopped salted nuts

Split the muffin with a fork; spread each half with butter mixed with the herbs and nuts. Put under broiler until edges are browned.

PASTRY MADE WITH OIL (*single crust*)

1⅓ cups sifted flour   ⅓ cup salad oil
½ teaspoon salt   2 tablespoons ice water

Sift flour and salt together into a bowl. Add oil and mix well with a fork. Sprinkle the water over it and mix again. Press dough together into a smooth ball, adding a bit more oil if the pastry is dry. Flatten; then roll out and handle as for the Traditional Method Pastry.

For a double-crust pie: Use 2 cups flour, 1 teaspoon salt, ½ cup oil, and 3 tablespoons ice water, following the same procedure as above. Divide dough into two parts before rolling out.

PASTRY MADE WITH INSTANT FLOUR (*single crust*)

1 cup instant-type flour   ⅓ cup plus 1 tablespoon
½ teaspoon salt   vegetable shortening
                    2 tablespoons ice water

Measure flour and salt into the small bowl of an electric mixer. Add shortening and mix at low speed about 1 minute, scraping the bowl and beater blades often. Add water, and continue mixing until all flour is moistened. If dough seems dry, add a teaspoon or two more of water. Shape dough into a ball, flatten, and roll out and bake as for Traditional Method Pastry.

For a double crust pie: Use 2 cups instant-type flour, 1 teaspoon salt, ¾ cup shortening, and ⅓ cup plus 1 tablespoon ice water.

TRADITIONAL METHOD PASTRY FOR ONE-CRUST PIE

1 cup sifted flour   ⅓ cup lard, or ⅓ cup plus
½ teaspoon salt   1 tablespoon vegetable
                                       shortening
                    2 to 3 tablespoons ice water

Sift flour and salt into bowl. With a pastry blender, two knives, or a broad-tined fork, cut the shortening into the flour until mixture resembles coarse crumbs. Sprinkle the cold water over it and mix lightly with a fork until pastry is just moist enough to hold together in a ball. It should not be sticky or so crumbly that it will not hold together. Shape into a smooth ball; flatten slightly and roll out on a lightly floured surface to fit the pie pan. Lay pastry loosely into the pan, but press out any air pockets. Crimp edges and trim off excess crust.

For a pie that requires an unbaked shell, just fill and bake. Or you can refrigerate the crust until needed. For pies that require a baked crust, prick evenly and closely over the entire surface of the pie pan. Refrigerate ½ hour before baking, while the oven is preheating. Bake the pie shell in a very hot oven (450°) for 10 to 15 minutes or until evenly golden brown. Watch it carefully so that it does not get too brown. Cool thoroughly before filling.

For a double-crust pie: Use 2 cups sifted flour, 1 teaspoon salt, ¾ cup vegetable shortening *or* ⅔ cup lard, and 4 to 5 tablespoons ice water. Follow the same procedure.

CREAM PUFFS

This recipe for cream puffs yields a dozen, but the extra ones can be frozen for later use when you need a quick dessert—especially for drop-in guests. Just fill the puffs with a scoop of ice cream or with whipped cream, and top with strawberries or chocolate syrup. To thaw quickly, put into a 400° oven for about 3 minutes.

1 cup water
¼ teaspoon salt
1 teaspoon sugar

½ cup (1 stick) butter or margarine
1 cup flour (all-purpose or instant-type)

4 eggs

Put water, salt, sugar, and butter into a saucepan, and heat until butter is melted. Bring mixture to a full rolling boil, and add the flour all at once; stir briskly until the flour absorbs all the liquid. Remove from heat, and beat until very smooth and pasty. Beat in the eggs, one at a time, until paste is smooth again and shiny. Let paste cool about 15 minutes before shaping and baking. Or put it into a plastic bag and refrigerate it until several hours later.

Shape paste into 12 balls, making them as high as possible for the most dramatic shape when they are baked. Use about ¼ cup of the paste for each puff, and place puffs 3 inches apart on a greased cookie sheet. Bake in a hot oven (400°) for 35 minutes or until golden and lightweight. To keep the shell crisp, poke a hole into each puff for steam to escape. Just before serving, fill with whipped cream, fruit, or ice cream, or use as directed in the chapter on "little main dishes." Makes 12 puffs.

*CREAM SCONES

Try these for breakfast with butter and jam.

1 cup flour	2 tablespoons butter
1½ teaspoons baking powder	1 egg, beaten
1 tablespoon sugar	2½ tablespoons heavy cream
¼ teaspoon salt	2 teaspoons sugar

Combine the flour, baking powder, sugar, and salt. With a fork, cut in the butter until the mixture resembles fine crumbs. Stir in the egg and cream to make a stiff dough. Turn out onto a board and knead lightly until dough sticks together. Pat into a 6-inch circle about 1 inch thick. With straight-edged knife, cut dough into 4 parts, making 4 wedge-shaped pieces. Place these on a greased cookie sheet and sprinkle with the sugar. Bake in a hot oven (400°) for 15 minutes or until golden. Serve immediately. Makes 4.

POPOVERS

Incredibly simple to make, and special pans are not needed!

½ cup flour, all-purpose or instant-type	1½ teaspoons melted butter or oil
⅛ teaspoon salt	½ cup milk
1 teaspoon sugar	1 large egg

Measure flour, salt, and sugar into a bowl or into blender container. Add the melted butter or oil, milk, and egg, and beat until smooth, scraping sides of bowl or container to be sure all flour is mixed in.

Grease baking cups (muffin cups or 5-ounce custard cups) very well. Fill about half full with batter. Bake in a 400° oven for about 35 to 40 minutes, until well browned and firm. Remove from pans and serve hot. Makes about 6 popovers.

Index

245